Style that Sizzles & Pacing for Power

An Editor's Guide to Writing Compelling Fiction

Jodie Renner

"This book is packed with good advice on how to spot and fix weaknesses in your fiction writing. It summarizes the combined wisdom of the last century or so of fiction teachers into one handy volume."

~ **Randy Ingermanson**, bestselling author of *Writing Fiction for Dummies*

"A handy checklist and self-editing guide that will get any fiction writer to a stronger, well-told tale."

~ **James Scott Bell**, bestselling author of *Revision & Self-Editing*, *Plot & Structure*, and *The Art of War for Writers*

Jodie Renner Editing
www.JodieRennerEditing.com

Cover Design: Travis Miles
www.probookcovers.com

Published by Cobalt Books, www.CobaltBooks.net

First published as an e-book on Amazon.com, September 2012
First Printing, March 2013, by CreateSpace

Printed in the United States of America
Also available in eBook publication

ISBN-13: 978-1481964715
ISBN-10: 1481964712

Library and Archives Canada Cataloguing in Publication

Renner, Jodie
Style that sizzles & pacing for power : an editor's guide
to writing compelling fiction / Jodie Renner.

Includes bibliographical references.
ISBN 978-1-4819-6471-5

1. Fiction--Authorship. 2. Fiction--Technique. I. Title.
II. Title: Style that sizzles and pacing for power.

PN3355.R446 2013 808.02 C2013-901001-7

Excerpts from Some of the Many 5-Star Reviews for
Style That Sizzles:

"*Style that Sizzles* is a book every fiction writer needs to have. I've read dozens of writing craft books, and this one is a gem. Jodie Renner addresses all the crucial issues and components in a novel and shows with great right-and-wrong examples how to trim and tighten your writing. [...] As a professional novelist, copyeditor, and writing coach, I can honestly say this comprehensive book covers everything a writer at any level needs to make a novel sizzle."

~ Susanne (C.S.) Lakin, writer and editor

"Jodie Renner's *Style that Sizzles & Pacing for Power* packs a knock-out punch in its 170 jewel-laden pages. This clearly written, access-friendly work provides the distilled wisdom of Jodie and multiple other fiction-writing gurus (James Scott Bell, Donald Maass, Sol Stein – just to name a few).

"*Sizzles* is the tightest and most useful collection of fiction writing tips and guidelines I have found. Whether you are starting your first book or deep in revision of your tenth, you will love this incredibly effective writing tool.

"I eagerly recommend this book. You will be pleased."

~ Tom Combs, MD

"Jodie Renner has achieved a remarkable feat here – she's distilled everything a fiction writer needs to know to draft edgy, compelling fiction into a short and sweet book. And she's done it by excluding all the fluff other craft books use as filler. [...] What's exceptionally useful is that the book is essentially a micro-manual for quick, easy-to-learn techniques to pare down your writing and make it lean and mean.

"Ms. Renner is the queen of thrillers and other crime fiction, but the invaluable advice provided here is applicable to anything you write, including non-fiction."

~ Eyeclocker

"Great news for fiction writers! Jodie Renner's *Style That Sizzles* has arrived! Before Jodie, self-editing was painful. After reading and using this book, I found it much easier – even fun – to go through my manuscripts and take out the trash. Her examples of her own editing are what did the trick for me, making her book the most useful writing guide I have run across yet. […] If you dream of writing a book that sells, buy this one to get you there faster!"

~ Kayak Writer

"There are many 'how to write fiction' books out there, but this is the only one I need for writing and editing my fiction. I feel everything I need to know to make my writing tight and compelling, I've found in this nice, compact, repository of great advice. [...] Maybe it's because she's an actual editor rather than another writer who has learned through the pitfalls of writing?

"The examples are clear and the writing is precise. It's exactly the kind of information I needed in a 'how to' book, and the knowledge that this author edits for a living makes this purchase well worth it to me."

~ Diane Carlisle

"This book packs in a wealth of tested how-to advice. Clearly, the author has a depth of personal experience in the writing craft. As a university tutor in fiction writing, I now recommend it to all my students. [...] It's written for the serious writer and goes quickly to the heart of what works, with plenty of real-world examples. Highly recommended."

~ Nigel J. Robinson, England

A few of Jodie's many testimonials for her fiction editing:

"Jodie Renner is a 5-star thriller editor with the eye of an eagle and the skill of a surgeon. She goes beyond copy and line editing to target even the most elusive content issues. A pleasure to work with – highly recommended.

~ Lynn Sholes & Joe Moore, Dec. 2012, #1 Amazon and international bestselling authors of *The Phoenix Apostles, The Grail Conspiracy,* and now, *The Blade.*

"When Jodie Renner says 'Let's take your manuscript to the next level,' she means it. […] Whether ratcheting up the tension, dealing with POV or timeline issues, grammar, or offering suggestions to enhance the plot, increase suspense, or pick up the pace, Jodie's suggestions are spot-on and invariably valuable. […] If you're looking for a way to set your work apart, look no farther than Jodie Renner Editing."

~ Allan Leverone, author of thrillers, mysteries and horror novels, Dec. 1, 2012. www.allanleverone.com

"Jodie Renner is the best editor you can hope for, because she pours her heart and soul into each project. […] with Jodie, weeding out typos, grammatical oversights, and clunky writing is just a small part of her work. She's a seasoned industry guru who will address both language and content issues to get your mystery, thriller, action, or espionage manuscript up to a publishable standard.

"Jodie will pore over every detail of your writing to transform it into a world-class novel that will sell. She will challenge every logical flaw and plot inconsistency in your story to ensure nothing comes in the way of your readers' suspension of disbelief."

~ A.M. Khalifa, thriller writer, Los Angeles, CA, February 2013

Acknowledgments

I'd like to thank bestselling author and writing guru, James Scott Bell, for taking the time to read this book and give me some valuable pointers for improving it. I have been reading Bell's excellent craft-of-writing books for years. His well-written, invaluable tips for writing a page-turner have guided my "big picture" fiction editing and informed me on current effective fiction techniques for my own craft-of-fiction articles and blog posts. Bell's books on writing fiction, especially *Revision & Self-Editing*, are at the top of my recommended reading lists for my aspiring author clients.

Randy Ingermanson, another highly respected writing teacher and co-author of the excellent starter book for aspiring fiction writers, *Writing Fiction for Dummies*, was also kind enough to read this book and offer encouragement and endorsement. Thank you so much, Randy!

A huge note of appreciation to author and editor par excellence, Jessica Page Morrell, who challenges us all by setting the bar so high for fiction writers and editors with her excellent books on the craft of writing and editing compelling stories. Jessica dispenses writing advice with attitude and sets the tone with her highly polished writing style and exemplary wordsmithing. Morrell's craft of writing books are chock-full of excellent advice for both writers and editors, and her *Thanks, But This Isn't For Us* was instrumental in helping me hone my skills as a copy editor and then dig deeper as a content editor. Jessica has been both a role model and a mentor to me in my editing and writing of craft articles and books.

Other fiction-writing gurus whose books I've devoured over the years include Donald Maass, Sol Stein, Stephen King, Jack M. Bickham, David Morrell, James N. Frey, Elizabeth Lyon, Hallie Ephron, Renni Browne & Dave King, Leigh Michaels, and more.

Finally, I'd like to thank my many writer clients – I've learned so much from editing your novels!

To my sons,

Jordan and Cory –

Thanks for your interest and support, guys!

TABLE OF CONTENTS

INTRODUCTION – WHAT WILL THIS BOOK DO FOR YOU?

If you want to produce a riveting, high-quality novel that sells, without spending a bundle on editing services, this book is for you. If you apply the easily accessible advice on these pages to revising and tightening your manuscript, you'll take your writing skills up a level or two and also end up saving a lot of money on editing costs.

The tips in this book, which grew out of my popular blog posts, are all about polishing your writing style and picking up the pace of a story you've already written, or are well into. But this advice, with frequent examples, will help any writer at any stage write tighter and stronger.

Not only will these pointers give you the tools to write more compelling fiction, but much of it also applies to publishing appealing blog posts, articles, and other writing. And you can apply these tips immediately to start honing your writing skills today, to hook more readers and increase your income.

For the purposes of this book, we'll assume that you've written a first draft of your story, or at least a third of it, and have already dealt with any major plot, characterization, point of view and other content and big-picture issues.

If not, check out my book, *Writing a Killer Thriller – An Editor's Guide to Writing Compelling Fiction*, which will help authors of any genre hone your craft, add tension, conflict and intrigue, and make your stories more captivating. I also have three more craft-of-fiction books in the works, which I hope you'll find helpful.

Now it's time to go back through your manuscript and cut or rewrite any boring scenes, then spiff up your writing style to produce a real page-turner that sells. In this book, you'll get concrete advice for revising and

1

editing your novel or short story until it's polished to a shine and ready to publish, right up there next to the best of them.

I'll help you show your scenes in real time, with action and dialogue, and give you concrete tips and examples for smoothing out clunky phrasing for better flow, by paring down any long, convoluted sentences to reveal their powerful core.

You'll learn how to swap out those overused, blah words for fresh, precise, powerful imagery. You'll get some great ideas for picking up the pace of your story and increasing the tension, for making your dialogue compelling and natural, and for finding your own authentic voice. Overall, you'll learn strategies for writing tighter to make every paragraph, sentence, and word count.

In addition, if you apply this advice to your current fiction manuscript, you'll also take your overall writing skills up several levels, which will make all your future writing projects more effortless and successful.

If you find this book helpful, I really hope you'll leave me a brief review on Amazon, under this book. If you have any questions or suggestions, please contact me directly at: info@JodieRennerEditing.com. I'd love to hear from you!

Also, for more information, check out my Amazon Author Page and my website, www.JodieRennerEditing.com.

Thank you, and keep on writing!

~ Jodie Renner, March 2013

PART I
WRITE TO ENGAGE

Chapter 1 – ZOOM OUT FIRST – SLASH OR FIX

THOSE BORING CHAPTERS & SCENES

Today's readers are much more impatient and discerning than readers of the past – and your competition is tough! Every chapter needs to grab your readers with lots of tension and intrigue and keep them turning the pages. There's no room for rambling or filler – each scene needs to advance the plot, complicate things, and reveal character.

You've written the first draft of your novel or at least half of it, and put it away for a week or three. Now step back and look at the forest rather than the trees. Do you have any chapters or scenes where nothing much really happens? Where there's not a lot of tension or intrigue? If so, your first job will be to evaluate, then rewrite, condense, or delete those scenes.

CUTTING OR REVISING LACKLUSTER CHAPTERS OR SCENES

Step 1: Evaluate every chapter and scene.

Pull back from the micro level of paragraphs, sentences and words, and critically assess the content of every chapter and scene to see if it's adding value or just getting in the way. You can use the Scene Outline Form in Appendix 1 to briefly summarize each scene in a sentence or two, so you can then look objectively at each one.

Step 2: Cut out irrelevant or boring scenes.

First, are there any chapters or scenes that can be deleted or saved for another story because they don't really enhance this one? Maybe they're going off on tangents with minor characters or subplots that don't tie in with this story or just complicate it. Or they're filler that's just reiterating or expanding on something you've already said. If so, take them out, even temporarily, and save them in another file. Reevaluate what's left. Is it clearer and stronger without that chapter / character / scene muddying the waters?

Step 3: Revise the remaining scenes to add tension, conflict and intrigue.

Check every scene that's left. Does it deepen characterization? Add conflict, suspense or intrigue? Advance the plot? If not, time to roll up your sleeves and get to work. Every scene needs conflict and a change: a revelation, challenge, victory, or setback. See my chapter, "Every Scene Needs Conflict and a Change" in *Writing a Killer Thriller – An Editor's Guide to Writing Powerful Fiction,* and my upcoming book, *Immerse the Reader in Your Story World.*

And important events need to be "shown" from the viewpoint of your protagonist or other major character, with action and dialogue, not "told" as in narrated (see Chapter 3, "Show, Don't Tell").

~ Put us in the head of your protagonist.

To deepen characterization and bring your scene to life, put your readers right inside the skin of your character, using deep point of view. For help with effective, compelling point of view techniques, see my articles, "POV 101: Get into Your Protagonist's Head – And Stay There for Most of Your Story," "POV 102: How to Avoid Head-Hopping," and "POV 103: Deep Point of View, or Close Third," at *The Writer's Forensics Blog.*

For more on ramping up your content and bringing your story and characters alive on the page, see my upcoming book, *Immerse the Reader in Your Story World – An Editor's Guide to Writing Compelling Fiction.*

Step 4: Amp up your writing style and pacing.

This is the main focus of this book. Within the scenes, are there passages that meander or stall out? Have you included too much exposition (explaining) or description? Those are often the parts that readers skim past, so best to reduce or eliminate them wherever possible. Same with backstory – filling in the character's history. Don't dump in this info in large lumps – marble it in on an "as needed" basis. Cut or condense any boring or repetitive parts in every paragraph, scene, and chapter. See Chapters 7–16.

Step 5: Revise paragraphs, sentences and words.

Here's where we start attacking convoluted sentence structure, wordiness, and repetition, and replacing weak word choices with more powerful ones. See chapters 13–16.

Step 6: Fine-tuning for details.

A final proofread for grammar, spelling, punctuation, capitalization, and spacing errors. For help with this, see my upcoming book, *The Final Polish – Putting the Finishing Touches on Your Novel*.

Step 7: Professional editing.

And of course, at some point, it's a very good idea to search out the services of a qualified freelance editor who reads and edits your genre. If you decide to go the indie publishing route, using a reputable freelance editor first will help ensure your novel meets industry standards and gets strong, positive reviews. Be sure to check out the editor's website, credentials and references, and get a sample edit of at least five pages first.

Chapter 2 – YOUR FIRST PAGES ARE CRITICAL

Gone are the days when fiction readers were willing to read pages of description and lead-up before being introduced to the characters and the plot. Readers, agents, and acquiring editors of today don't have the time or patience to wade through pages of backstory and description, so you need to grab their interest right from the first sentence and first paragraph of your story.

As James Scott Bell says in *Revision and Self-Editing*, about the opening paragraphs, "Give us a character in motion. Something happening to a person from line one. Make that a disturbing thing, or have it presage something disturbing."

TWELVE DOS AND DON'TS FOR AN OPENING THAT HOOKS READERS IN

1. Don't begin with a long description of the setting or with background information on your main character.

Do begin with dialogue and action; then add any necessary backstory or description in small doses, on a need-to-know basis as you progress through the story.

2. Don't start with a character other than your protagonist.

Do introduce your protagonist right in the first paragraph. Readers want to know right away whose story it is, which character you're asking them to identify with.

3. Don't start with a description of past events.

Do jump right in with what the main character is involved in *right now*, and introduce some tension or conflict as soon as possible.

4. Don't start in a viewpoint other than the main character's.

Do start telling the story from your protagonist's point of view, so readers start bonding with him or her right away. It's best to stay in the protagonist's viewpoint for the whole first chapter, or most of it, and don't change the point of view within a scene.

5. Don't introduce your protagonist in a static, neutral (boring) situation.

Do develop your main character quickly by putting her in a bit of hot water and showing how she reacts to the situation, so readers can empathize and "bond" with her, and start caring enough about her to keep reading.

6. Don't start with your character all alone, reflecting on his life.

Do have more than one character (two is best) interacting, with action and dialogue. That's more compelling than reading the thoughts of one person.

7. Don't start with your protagonist planning a trip or traveling somewhere.

In other words, don't start them on their way to an important scene. Do start *in medias res* — jump right into the middle of the action. Present her in a meaningful scene.

8. Don't introduce a lot of characters in the first few pages.

Do limit the number of characters you introduce in the first few pages to three or less.

9. Don't leave the reader wondering what the characters look like.

Do provide a brief description of each character as they're introduced, or as soon as you can work it in, so the readers can form a picture of him or her in their minds. But don't spend too much time detailing every single thing they're wearing – a rough sketch is best, with first-impression character traits, and from your viewpoint character's point of view.

10. Best to avoid having the main character looking in the mirror.

This had been overdone as a device for describing your protagonist. Do work in the description by relating it to their thoughts, attitude, actions or interactions with others, or use the reactions of another character toward them.

11. Don't wait too long to introduce the love interest or villain.

To add interest and intrigue, in a romance, do introduce the hero (love interest) and, in a thriller, show us the antagonist (bad guy) within the first chapter or two.

12. Don't spend too long on setup.

Don't take chapters to introduce the main conflict or problem the protagonist faces.

Do write in an inciting incident, or at least some significant tension, within the first chapter.

Remember, you can always start your story wherever you want in the draft stage, if it'll make you feel better. Then in the editing stage, you can go back and cut out the first several paragraphs or pages or even most of the first chapter or two, so that, in your final draft, your actual story starts after all that lead-up (some of which may appear later, in snippets here and there).

In conclusion, here's a little rule for writing compelling fiction, coined by James Scott Bell:

Act first, explain later.

Resources:
James Scott Bell, *Revision & Self-Editing*
Other reading
Jodie's editing

Chapter 3 – SHOW, DON'T TELL

"SHOW, DON'T TELL" is the most familiar mantra among advisors to fiction writers, and one of the most difficult concepts for new fiction writers to grasp. Mastering this concept will make a huge difference in the quality of your stories.

What does it mean? It's about bringing the scene to life and putting the reader right there, inside your character, experiencing her fear along with her, feeling the sweat on his brow and his adrenaline racing, your pulse quickening right along with theirs, muscles tensed, ready to leap into action.

CUT BACK ON NARRATION, DESCRIPTION, AND EXPOSITION

Remember this: **Story trumps all.** Keep the story moving and the characters interacting. The author stepping in to describe or explain things to the readers brings the story to a screeching halt and can be distracting, boring or irritating for readers. For more on this, see Chapter 8.

DON'T *TELL* US WHAT HAPPENED – *SHOW* US WHAT HAPPENED

A common mistake among aspiring fiction writers is to describe or narrate (tell) events as if they took place at some point in the past, instead of putting the reader right in the middle of the action and showing the events as they occur, in real time, along with the characters' actions, reactions, inner thoughts and feelings, and actual words (direct dialogue in quotations).

To clarify what is meant by "show, don't tell," think of it this way: Which

11

would you rather do, go see a great movie in a theatre with a big screen and surround sound ("show"), or hear about the movie from someone else afterward ("tell")? That's the difference we're talking about here.

Janet Evanovich considers "show, don't tell" to be one of the most important principles of fiction: "Instead of stating a situation flat out, you want to let the reader discover what you're trying to say by watching a character in action and by listening to his dialogue. Showing brings your characters to life."

DON'T GET IN THE WAY OR INTERPRET FOR US

We like to experience things for ourselves, not hear about them from someone else. Think about watching those slide shows with narration, from your neighbors' vacation. Yawn. In the same way, readers of popular fiction don't want to be kept at arm's length, to be told what's happening by an intermediary narrator. They want to experience the events firsthand, to see, hear and feel what's happening. They want to feel the character's fears, hopes, joys and worries and draw their own conclusions.

As Jack Bickham says, "Not only does moment-by-moment development make the scene seem most lifelike, it's in a scene [with dialogue and action and reaction] where your reader gets most of his excitement. If you summarize, your reader will feel cheated – short-changed of what he reads for – without quite knowing why."

It's through characters interacting that a scene comes alive, so put us right there with the characters, in the middle of the tension and conflict, using "live" action and dialogue.

ALSO, NO NEED TO "TELL" AFTER YOU'VE "SHOWN"

Before:
"You're late!" the general said. **He didn't like to be kept waiting.**

Don't explain after the fact. The words and actions should convey it.

After:
"You're late!" the general said, glaring at him, hands on hips.

Other no-no examples of telling after showing. In each case, take out the unnecessary sentence at the end:

She moped around the house and wouldn't answer the phone. Even TV didn't interest her. **She was depressed**.

"You crack me up," she said, laughing hysterically. **Joel could be so funny**.

USE DEEP POINT OF VIEW

Use close third-person point of view (or first person) to put us right into your protagonist's or other main character's head and skin. Show us her thoughts, reactions, and plans, his inner fears, hopes, resentments, anger, confusion, tenderness, relief, and joy. Don't keep the reader at arm's length by describing your hero or heroine from the outside, using omniscient or distant third-person point of view.

EVOKE ALL FIVE SENSES

Showing means presenting the story to the reader using sensory information. The reader wants to *feel* what the character is feeling, experience their fear, joy, anger, determination, and pain, know their inner hopes and thoughts, and also *see* what's happening, *hear* the different voices of the characters and other sounds, *smell* the smells, *feel* the tactile sensations, and *taste* the food and drink along with them. *Telling*, on the other hand, is summarizing the story for the reader in a way that skips past the evocative, life-giving sensory information and just relates the basic actions and events that occurred.

USE POWERFUL, EVOCATIVE PHRASING

As Jessica Morrell says, "adjectives *tell* and verbs *show*. For example, instead of *shiny necklace*, trade the adjective *shiny* for a verb: *the necklace glinted* or *the necklace sparkled, gleamed, flashed, glimmered,*

13

shimmered, twinkled." Instead of "the miner was *tired*" (telling) say "the miner *trudged* home, head bowed," or "the miner *plodded* along, his boots feeling like lead weights" or "the miner *clomped* over the gravel with heavy steps." Or s*logged* or *tramped* or *lumbered* or *dragged* or *shuffled* (showing).

Do a search for the word "was" – it's often an indicator of telling instead of showing, as in "she was sad" or "he was angry." Show their feelings instead by their thoughts, actions, words, tone, and body language.

ADD IN LOTS OF TENSION AND CONFLICT

Also, the bulk of the scene needs to be about a conflict of some kind between characters. No conflict = no scene. According to Jack Bickham, the conflict part of the scene "draws readers out through a moment-by-moment drama, extending the scene suspense with pleasurable agony."

RECAP – TIPS FOR SHOWING
INSTEAD OF TELLING

~ Show the characters' actions as they're occurring, in real time.

~ Use deep point of view to get right into the skin, head and heart of your character.

~ Show us your viewpoint character's reactions, feelings, emotions, and thoughts.

~ Add in sensory information. What are they seeing, hearing, touching, tasting, feeling?

~ Include lots of spirited, to-the-point dialogue.

~ Look for "was" or "were" and rephrase the sentence, replacing the adjective with a compelling verb or verbal phrase.

~ Cut way back on narrative description, exposition, and lengthy explanations of the character's past or motivations.

~ Keep flashbacks short, and show them in real time, with action and dialogue.

~ Throw in plenty of conflict and tension.

~ Avoid telling after you've shown.

EXAMPLES OF SHOWING, RATHER THAN TELLING

Telling: Jake's words spooked me.

Showing: The hair on my arms rose when I thought about Jake's words.

Telling: George was disgusted and angry.

Showing: George pounded his fist on the table and swore at her, his lips curling. "Don't ever do that again."

Telling: Janie was bored at her Grandma's.

Showing: Janie wandered from room to room, trying to find something to do. She wished it wasn't raining outside. She looked through Grandma's old books but nothing interested her.

BUT "TELL" TO SUMMARIZE – OR SKIP RIGHT PAST – THE BORING BITS

Of course, you can't show everything, or your book would be way too long, and it would tire your readers out – or worse, end up boring them. According to James Scott Bell, "Sometimes a writer tells as a shortcut, to move quickly to the meaty part of the story or scene. Showing is essentially about making scenes vivid. If you try to do it constantly, the parts that are supposed to stand out won't, and your readers will get exhausted." Telling or summarizing is useful for relating something quickly, for skipping over time and past boring bits.

The rule, says Bell, is "the more intense the moment, the more showing you do." That's the difference between scene and summary. You don't want to describe every move your characters make at down times, or when going from one place to the other. That's where you summarize or "tell," to get them to the next important scene quickly, without a lot of boring detail.

The main thing to keep in mind is to *never tell the reader, after the fact* (or have a character telling another character), *about a critical scene. Instead, dramatize it in the here and now,* with dialogue, action, and lots of sensory details to bring it to life for the reader.

Resources:
James Scott Bell, *Revision & Self-Editing*
Jack M. Bickham, *The 38 Most Common Fiction Writing Mistakes*
Randy Ingermanson & Peter Economy, *Writing Fiction for Dummies*
Jessica Page Morrell, *Thanks, But This Isn't For Us*
And Jodie's editing and critical reading of bestsellers

Chapter 4 – BRING YOUR CHARACTERS TO LIFE BY SHOWING THEIR REACTIONS

Readers want to escape into your story world. They want to immerse themselves in your story and vicariously experience what your protagonist is experiencing. Your character's reactions to what's going on around them are what make the situation seem real and the character more charismatic, vulnerable and multi-dimensional. If your character's reactions feel natural and believable to the reader, they will quickly suspend disbelief and become emotionally invested. They'll be turning the pages with satisfaction.

So in order to bring your POV (point of view) characters (main characters) to life on the page and make the readers start to worry about them, it's critical to constantly show the characters' reactions to what's happening to and around them. If you just describe events and skip over or minimize characters' reactions to what's going on, the characters will seem flat, boring, emotionless – or worse, cold and unfeeling.

BE SURE TO SHOW YOUR CHARACTERS' REACTIONS

As Jack M. Bickham says, "Readers want to know how your characters feel about what's happening to them, and want to see their response to the words and actions of others and events unfolding around them."

Here's a scene I just made up quickly where a father needs to react more:

> David just got back to his office when the phone rang. It was his wife. "Hi, hon. What's up?"
> "Finally! I've been trying to reach you for hours. Cassie's missing! She didn't show up at school today and her bed hasn't been slept in! She's not answering her cell phone and none of her friends have seen her today. I need you. Can you get here

right away?"

"All right, I'll be there soon." He grabbed his coat and told the receptionist he'd be gone for the rest of the day.

On the way home, he tried to convince himself there was a good reason for his fourteen-year-old daughter's absence.

Not only does this guy not seem to care much about his daughter or be all that concerned that she's missing, which unintentionally paints him in a bad light, his lack of reaction makes for boring reading, too.

BUT DON'T OVERDO IT

But do make sure the reaction actually fits the situation and is in keeping with the character's personality and motivations. Cold, stoic, unfeeling characters won't draw your reader in (unless it's the villain), but neither will constant emoting, gushing, wailing, raging, or gnashing of teeth. See Chapter 5 for more on this.

HAVE THEM REACT IMMEDIATELY, AS THEY WOULD IN REAL LIFE

To bring your character to life on the page, have him or her react right away to exciting, frustrating, shocking, frightening, or stressful events. Don't delay the reaction. Immediately following the stressful stimulus, show your POV character's visceral reaction and/or a short, vehement thought-reaction, like *Oh no!* or *No way!* Or *You're kidding.* Or *Oh my god.* Or *Idiot!* Or *What the hell?* or *You wish.* Or *What a hunk!* Or *Damn.* (Or another swear word.) Or by some other quick emotional or physical reaction.

Two sisters are jogging in the park, deep in conversation, when a loud horn behind them makes them jump. Show them jumping (automatic reflex) with maybe a verbal expletive, then looking back and laughing or whatever, before the cyclist passes with a wave or a laugh or a curse, and then they shake their heads and resume their conversation.

The visceral reaction of your POV character and her immediate thought-reaction or surprised cry or swear word will make the scene more real to the readers. This is also "show, don't tell." Telling would be "The horn

18

surprised them and made them jump. Then they continued talking." Show their reactions in a more compelling, right-there way.

SHOW THE REACTIONS IN THEIR NATURAL ORDER

It's important to show your character's visceral reaction to a situation first, before an overt action or words. And show involuntary thought-reactions or word-reactions before more reasoned thought processes and decision-making, which lead to more considered, thoughtful words and conscious actions.

As Ingermanson and Economy put it, "Here's a simple rule to use: **Show first whatever happens fastest.**

Most often, this means you show interior emotion first, followed by various instinctive actions or dialogue, followed by the more rational kinds of action, dialogue, and interior monologue."

AND DON'T SKIP THOSE FIRST STEPS!

Remember, we're inside that character's head and body, so you'll deepen their character and draw us closer to them by showing us what they're feeling immediately inside – those involuntary physical and thought reactions that come before controlled, civilized outward reactions.

Jack Bickham points out that credibility results from understanding **the stages of response**. Character reaction, like human reaction in general, has four individual parts. As writers, we don't necessarily have to put all four on the page at any given point in time, but any reactions we do show should be stated in the order they occur.

First, show the stimulus that has caused them to react.

Then show some or all of these responses, in this order:

1. The character's **visceral response** – adrenaline surging, pulse racing, stomach clenching, heart pounding, mouth drying, flushing, shivering, cold skin, tense muscles, sweating, blushing, shakiness, etc.

2. Their **unconscious knee-jerk physical action** – yelling, gasping, crying out, snatching hand or foot away from source of heat or pain, striking out, etc.

3. Their **thought processes** and decision to act

4. Their **conscious action** or verbal response

If we violate that order, we're depriving the reader of an opportunity to get further into the head and skin of that character, to feel what they're feeling, to be right there with them. And the reader may subconsciously feel disappointed that we didn't give them a more complete picture, or they'll wonder how the character really felt, how the event really affected them inside.

We also risk creating a tiny, niggling disquiet in the mind of our readers, a sense that there is something wrong, and that disconnect can bump them out of the story.

Also, see Chapter 26 – Expressing Thought-Reactions in Fiction.

Resources:
Jodie's editing and critical reading of fiction
Jack M. Bickham, *The 38 Most Common Fiction Writing Mistakes*
Randy Ingermanson and Peter Economy, *Writing Fiction for Dummies*

Chapter 5 – SHOW EMOTIONS, BUT DON'T BE MELODRAMATIC

While it's important to bring your fictional characters to life on the page by showing their feelings and reactions to what's going on around them, be careful not to go overboard and slip into melodrama, which can be a real turn-off for readers.

~ What is Melodrama?

According to Merriam-Webster's online dictionary, it is "characterized by extravagant theatricality" and writing that has "a sensational or theatrical quality."

Another term for roughly the same idea – exaggeration of emotionally reactions to circumstances – is "**purple prose**."

Dictionary.com defines purple prose as "writing that calls attention to itself because of its obvious use of certain effects, as exaggerated sentiment or pathos, especially in an attempt to enlist or manipulate the reader's sympathies."

According to Sol Stein, "'Purple prose' means writing that is overblown. It turns off editors and readers almost immediately." Stein gives these examples of purple prose:

"The cry of a soul in torment, swept by a tide of anger and outrage."

"Jagged laughter tore at her throat."

"Ghastly red spatterings, viscous red-streaked gobbets of his brains."

So your job as a fiction writer is to say just enough to stimulate emotions in the reader. We certainly don't want flat characters who don't feel or react to things, but excessive emoting, whether it's gushing, wailing, or hand-wringing, turns off the readers, just as it does people in life.

~ Examples of Melodrama:

Here are a few disguised examples from my fiction editing of going overboard, with names and circumstances altered to ensure anonymity.

In the first example of melodramatic writing, Jan and her friend Alicia discover their colleague, Tom, dead in his office. Alicia, who is new there, just met the man the day before.

> Jan touched Tom's neck and felt for a pulse. There was none.
> "He's dead!" Jan shrieked, tears erupting and pouring down her face.
> Alicia started to wail. It was a piercing howl that seemed to emanate from deep within her soul. Jan turned and grabbed her. She held her tight, her own cries of desperation joining her friend's.

Bear in mind that they're all just colleagues, and Alicia had barely met the victim. These reactions are way over the top for the death of a co-worker and new acquaintance.

And this one, too, is way overdone and needs to be toned down:

> "Oh my God!" Christine shrieked. The killer was looking for me—not Kyle.
> The words screamed in her mind. The realization that she was the target was too much for Christine to handle. She lost all control. Her anguished cries shattered the silence, sounding like an injured wild animal in the final throes of an excruciating death. Christine covered her face with her hands as her cries of despair reverberated from deep within her body. The feeling of desperation was worse than anything she had ever experienced.

Again, way, way over the top. Don't hammer the readers over the head with an emotional sledgehammer. Subtle is very often more effective. Let the readers draw on their own experience to supply some of the specifics of the grief, rather than overwhelming them with too much emotion.

When the writing is trying too hard to impress the readers or make them feel sympathy for the characters, it crosses the line over into melodrama, and can feel manipulative to the reader. It's best to ferret out these overdone passages and "kill your darlings" (see below) to retain your readers.

~ Don't Shoot Your Wad

Don't overuse powerful words in situations where they're not needed or warranted. Then when you really need them, they'll have lost their power from overuse in minor situations. Save strong words like *horrifying, excruciating, terrified, ecstatic, frantic, frenzied, blissful,* and *shocking* for when they're really needed and justified.

Before:
> Gayle parked and made her way into the mall, where she joined the **horde of frantic Christmas shoppers**. She shook her head at the **frenzied mob**.

Christmas shopping can be a trial, but shoppers aren't usually frantic, and they're definitely not a "frenzied mob"? (At least not usually!) What about when you really need the words "mob" or "frantic" or "frenzied"? They won't have the power you're looking for because they've been overused to describe fairly ordinary situations.

After:
> Gayle parked and made her way into the mall, where she joined the **throng of busy Christmas shoppers**. She shook her head at the **rushing crowd**.

~ Less is more.

Often in effective fiction writing, less is more, and that applies to expressing emotional reactions as well. So it's usually better to use fewer adjectives, less flowery or overwrought emotional description, and more action and dialogue to convey the emotions.

But don't worry about censuring yourself in your first draft. Go ahead and express the emotions freely the first time through, then when you go back to revise it, step back and look at it from the reader's point of view. If it seems over the top, look for ways to tone it down a bit.

~ "Kill Your Darlings"

If a phrase, sentence or paragraph draws attention to itself, that's usually an indication that it should be revised or even deleted. In fact, if you're particularly proud of a turn of phrase, that could be an indication that it might just be a bit too much.

That's where the saying, "Kill your darlings" comes from – phrases you've fallen in love with that may not really fit there at all. They're just there because you slaved over them and you like them.

By all means, keep them if they advance the plot or deepen characterization and seem realistic and natural, but maybe toned down a bit. If not, save them on another file for future use elsewhere, like in a different genre. At the very least, run them past your critique group and ask for their honest opinions.

Resources:
Jodie's editing and
Sol Stein, *Stein on Writing*

Chapter 6 – STIMULUS AND RESPONSE – PHRASING FOR IMMEDIACY AND POWER

Have you ever been engrossed in a novel, reading along, then you hit a blip that made you go "huh?" for a nanosecond? Then you had to reread the sentence to figure out what's going on? Often, it's because actions are written in a jumbled-up order, rather than the order they actually occurred. When writing fiction, it's usually best to show actions and events in chronological order, and to describe the cause first, then the effect. Something happens, then the character reacts to it, not the other way around.

So when showing actions and reactions in your fiction, pay attention to the syntax of the sentence. State the cause before the effect, the action before the reaction, the stimulus before the response. This way, the ideas flow more naturally and smoothly, and the readers don't have to skip back in the sentence to figure out what's going on, which confuses them momentarily and takes them out of the story.

STATE CAUSE before EFFECT, ACTION before REACTION, STIMULUS before RESPONSE

As Ingermanson and Economy say, "Here's a critical rule:

"Always get the time sequence correct and always put the cause before the effect."

Here are some "before and after" examples, disguised, from my fiction editing. The "after" examples are just one or two of many possibilities.

Instead of:

David yelled out in pain when the door slammed on his fingers.

Write:
> The door slammed on David's fingers and he yelled out in pain.

Or:
> The door slammed on David's fingers. He leaped back, yelling out in pain.

Instead of:

> She pulled her arm away when the man tried to grab her.

Write:
> The man tried to grab her, but she pulled her arm away.

Or:
> The man tried to grab her arm, but she pulled away.

DESCRIBE PHYSICALLY SEQUENTIAL ACTIONS IN THE ORDER THEY OCCURRED

Instead of:

> Jake walked the five hundred yards over to the police station and left his car in front of the restaurant.

Write:
> Jake left his car in front of the restaurant and walked the five hundred yards over to the police station.

Instead of:

> Boyd jumped out of the car as he reached the parking lot and ran into the bar.

Write:
> Boyd raced into the parking lot, jumped out of the car, and ran into the bar.

If you don't write the actions in the order they occurred, it causes momentary confusion for the reader. Do that enough and they start getting subliminally annoyed.

USE WITH CAUTION: –ING VERBS, AS, AND

~ Be careful when using –ing verbs:

Avoid using the way-too-common "ing" verbs for actions that occur one after the other. Verbs ending in -ing imply simultaneous action where there is none:

Instead of:

She slammed the car door, running up the sidewalk.

Write:
She slammed the car door, then ran up the sidewalk.

Instead of:

He took out his keys, starting the car.

Write:
He took out his keys and started the car.

In the "before" examples above, the –ing verbs imply that the actions occurred at the same time, which is impossible—she can't run up the sidewalk as she's slamming the door. He can't start the car while he's taking out his keys.

Or even worse:

Slamming on the brakes, she raced for the front door.

If you describe too many physically impossible action combinations like that, the reader is likely to throw your book across the room in disgust.

~ Watch the use of "as" – be sure it actually works there:

Before:

He suppressed a shiver **as** the night's cold clung in the early morning air.

The sentence doesn't really work with the "as" there.

After:
The night's cold clung in the early morning air, making him shiver.

~ "And" can sometime be problematic, too:

Before:
In front of the store, a little boy wore a red jacket **and** held the hand of a blond-haired woman.

With the verb-plus-*and*-plus-verb as it is above, it's like two separate actions occurring.

After:
In front of the store, a little boy wearing a red jacket held the hand of a blond-haired woman.

THINK THROUGH ACTION OR FIGHT SCENES

Writing so that one action happens after another, in a logical sequence, makes for a smoother, more natural, flow of ideas. This can be especially troublesome for fight scenes or chases, where so much is happening that it's easy for the readers to get confused. For example:

Before: In this scene as it was originally written, the sequence of events is unclear and out of order, with essential actions missing.

Another officer leaped from a second PD unit that had been following dogging the two officers, taking the stance with a drawn gun aimed at the pickup. Kirk slammed the truck in reverse and gunned the engine, knocking down the officer behind him, dragging him as he smashed the gears into drive, then gunning it forward using the truck as a battering weapon. Just then a delivery truck parked at the far end of the alley. Kirk slammed the truck in reverse seeing the end of the alley blocked by the delivery truck.

After: As it's written below, it's much easier to visualize what's going on:

Another officer leaped from a second PD unit that had been dogging the two officers. He sprinted toward the alley, then took the stance with a drawn gun aimed at the pickup. Kirk slammed the truck in reverse and gunned the engine, knocking down the officer behind him, then smashed the gears into drive and gunned it forward, dragging him along as he used the truck as a battering weapon. Just then a delivery truck parked at the far end of the alley. Seeing the end of the alley blocked by the delivery truck, Kirk slammed the truck in reverse again.

BUT BREAK THE RULE OCCASIONALLY
FOR SUSPENSE

To add more suspense and intrigue, occasionally it's effective to show a character's reaction to something shocking before describing what she is reacting to. In this case, you'll create a more dramatic effect if you have your character react first, and then show what it is she's seeing.

This way, you'll have a moment of suspense between the horrified reaction and the revelation of what's being seen. Also, it may take a paragraph or more to describe what she's seeing, so her reaction would be delayed, which can be a bit anticlimactic.

The beam of her flashlight scanned the floor ahead. She stopped and gasped in horror.

Calvin lay on the concrete, his eyes starting unseeing at the ceiling. Blood spattered the floor around him. His throat had been slit from ear to ear.

Resources:
Jodie's editing
Ingermanson & Economy, *Writing Fiction for Dummies*

Chapter 7 – IT'S A STORY, NOT AN INSTRUCTION MANUAL!

Fiction writing is all about sucking your readers in and keeping them eagerly turning the pages to find out what happens next, so be careful not to put any roadblocks or speed bumps in their way. Here are some tips for keeping the story flowing, rather than bumping readers out of it by frustrating them, even subliminally.

DON'T GET TOO TECHNICAL ABOUT WHICH HAND OR FOOT OR...

Whether you're writing an action scene or a love scene, it's best not to get too technical or clinical about which hand or leg or finger or foot is doing what, unless it's relevant or necessary for understanding.

Getting bogged down in details is distracting to the reader and can even be laughable or annoying. Of course we want to know what's going on and how the characters are feeling, but we don't need a highly detailed, anatomical description of every little gesture and movement.

Without getting too far into the bedroom, here's kind of an extreme example of way too much detail, off the top of my head:

He stroked her left forearm and wrist with his right index finger, while his left thumb brushed aside a strand of hair from her right eye and tucked it behind her right ear.

All that precision is totally unnecessary and way too distracting. And if we were to move into the bedroom, there's nothing that kills a love scene faster than detailed, clinical descriptions of exactly which of various appendages and other body parts are doing what, in what order, and how. Keep the instruction manuals out of the bedroom!

Similarly, in an action scene or a fight, unless we really need to know, for logistic reasons, which hand, arm, or leg is doing what, don't bother specifying, as it slows down the action and can be distracting, even annoying.

Here are some examples, altered and disguised from various stories I've edited:

Before:
> His father yanked the earbuds out of Jeff's ears **with his left hand** and grabbed his iPod **with his right hand**. "Listen to me when I'm talking to you!"

We don't really need to know which hand is doing each action. Take out the unnecessary details and what is left is stronger:

After:
> His father yanked the earbuds out Jeff's ears and grabbed his iPod. "Listen to me when I'm talking to you!"

Before:
> Cory **used his hands to** frantically push the boxes away from the opening, then clambered through it.

There's no need to specify that he used his hands – what else would he push the boxes away with?

After:
> Cory frantically pushed the boxes away from the opening, then clambered through it.

Before:
> He looked quickly at Jack, **who dropped his arm holding** the gun and gave a purposeful glance **first to his left and then his right**. He looked back **in their direction**, stared fiercely for a moment, and began walking calmly, slowly, towards them.

After:
> He looked at Jack, who lowered the gun and glanced both ways. He glared back at them for a moment, then began walking slowly towards them.

And while we're at it, no need to say "He nodded his head," or "She shrugged her shoulders." What else would he nod? What else would she shrug? Just say "He nodded," and "She shrugged."

It's best to avoid having unnecessary details that just add clutter.

DON'T HAVE BODY PARTS DOING DISEMBODIED THINGS

Don't have renegade body parts acting independently of the rest of the body, for example, "His hand reached for the cup of coffee." That feels weird, like the hand detached itself from his body or just decided to act on its own. "He reached for the cup of coffee" sounds much more natural.

Before:
> "Hey, Matt, take that left and we can come at them from the other side." **Greg's hands indicated** an alleyway off to the left. Matt turned the vehicle and took off down the alley.

After:
> "Hey, Matt, take that left and we can come at them from the other side." **Greg pointed to** an alleyway off to the left. Matt the vehicle and took off down the alley.

And you don't need to say that someone's hand or finger pointed in a direction – what else do people normally point with?

Instead of "She **pointed her finger at** the car," Just say, "She **pointed at** the car."

AND DON'T HAVE EYES PERFORMING IMPOSSIBLE ACTIONS

These days, agents, editors and readers frown on oddly phrased sentences to express how someone is looking at someone else, like in these examples:

> "Cathy walked into the ward. Before her eyes landed on the patient, she heard the blaring of a television set."

"His eyes bounced back and forth between them." (boing, boing, boing)

"Her eyes shot daggers at him." (Ow! Ow!)

"She dropped her eyes to the floor." (splat!)

"Her eyes clung to his." (like Velcro)

"He devoured her with his eyes." (munch, munch)

"Her eyes darted across the room." (speedy)

"Her eyes fell to her lap." (cushioned fall, at least)

It's too easy for readers to form a comical mental picture of eyeballs popping out of someone's head and doing strange things, and start thinking it's some kind of parody. So it's best to do a search for the words "eyes" in your story, and if they're doing weird things, see if you can find a more subtle, natural way of expressing how the characters are looking at each other.

Often, just replacing "eyes" with "gaze" will solve the problem:

Not: "His eyes followed her across the room."

But: "His gaze followed her across the room."

Chapter 8 – INFO DUMPS, LECTURES, AYKB, & OTHER AUTHOR INTRUSIONS

DON'T JOLT US OUT OF YOUR STORY

Have you ever been reading a novel when suddenly the author interrupts the story to give you technical information about something? Or introduces a new character, then spends the next several paragraphs or even pages giving you way more detail than you need or want at this point about their background, upbringing, education, qualifications, work experience, and relationships?

Or maybe, in the guise of fiction, the author starts waxing eloquent about a pet cause of theirs? Or they try to sneak in some info via a dialogue, only it's really a monologue, with a character going on for a half page or more, uninterrupted, lecturing about something? Fortunately, this rarely happens to this extent anymore. Unlike a hundred years ago, today's readers of fiction won't stand for this kind of heavy-handed, clunky imparting of information within a story.

Keep the story going!

Savvy authors know that readers choose fiction to be entertained and swept away by a compelling story. Stopping to fill them in on a topic or somebody's history jars them out of the story, slows down the pace, and runs the risk of boring and annoying them. If readers want to find out more information on a subject, they can do that very easily these days, through internet searches.

So unless you're writing a historical saga like *Hawaii* by James Michener or *New York* by Edward Rutherfurd, where readers welcome background info on historically relevant times and locations, fiction is not the place to interrupt the story to insert a lot of detail on a particular subject. And of course, if you are writing a saga, it's best to include the info in a natural, character-specific way, so it doesn't come across like a history textbook. (See below for some hints.)

So when you're revising your novel, be on the lookout for any obvious blocks of information or mini-lectures that you may have inadvertently wedged into the story here and there.

Author intrusions and info dumps come in various shapes and sizes, but whatever their form, they can be perceived as an obvious and clumsy attempt by the author to quickly impart some facts, clarifications, or personal opinions directly to the reader.

It might even be considered lazy – it's much easier to just insert a bunch of backstory in about a character in one lump, for example, than to find ways to artfully weave in the most important points through dialogue and thoughts, etc. And do we really need *all* of that information on the character, anyway? Definitely not at the risk of turning off your reader, who's just been wrenched out of the story to be filled in on résumé-like background info.

So be careful not to dump a bunch of factual information willy-nilly into your story. A novel or short story is no place to go into a lot of detail on a technical subject – or to get on your soapbox about a topic that's dear to your heart or makes your blood boil. Readers will feel annoyed, patronized or manipulated, when what they really want is to be entertained and captivated by your tale.

WHY SHOULDN'T I EXPLAIN THINGS
TO THE READERS?

Here's why most readers of contemporary fiction don't like having their story interrupted by author explanations:

~ It takes them out of the character's viewpoint, so the illusion of being right there in the character's head and their story world is shattered.

~ It creates a jarring interruption to the story line, which you then have to re-establish, and hook your readers back in.

~ Readers may feel you're lecturing them or preaching to them, which has no place in fiction.

~ It's distracting, annoying, and often boring.

SOME COMMON TYPES OF AUTHOR INTRUSIONS TO AVOID

~ INFO DUMPS – Stopping the Story to Explain Information at Length to Your Readers

Readers like to stay immersed in the story, not be pulled out of it to be given a lengthy explanation of something as an aside by the author. This can include long, detailed explanations of a specific type of gun, for example, or stopping the story to describe in detail how fingerprints are retrieved, processed, analyzed, and fed into data systems.

Yes, do your research, for sure. But pick and choose what you actually share with your readers, and blend the info in in a natural way, through dialogue, introspection and short expository (explaining) passages, filtered through the attitude, circumstances, and knowledge base of the point of view (POV) character or revealed in the course of dialogue, preferably with some tension and dissension thrown in.

For an excellent example of how to impart information while staying in the story and entertaining your readers at the same time, see my excerpt at the end of this chapter from Robert Crais's thriller, *The Last Detective*.

~ SOAP-BOXING ABOUT AN ISSUE OR CAUSE

Maybe you'd like to increase consciousness about worthy topics such as the plight of whales or the lack of clean water worldwide, or unfair treatment of minorities, or lack of green spaces. You say, "But people really need to be made aware of the situation – we all need to sit up and take notice and do something about it!"

That's very true, but you could always write letters to the editor or newspaper or magazine articles on the issue, or start a blog dedicated to the issue, or contribute to online magazines and blogs. Or join special interest groups or volunteer or give talks at the library or to local groups.

And sure, insert allusions to social issues here and there in your novel, as long as you have a character who is passionate about that issue and knowledgeable. It can work in small doses, as long as you don't go on so long about it that it comes across as preaching. And of course it needs to fit naturally in the scene and reflect the character's personality, politics and thoughts.

~ PONTIFICATING – Giving the Readers a History Lesson or a Lecture on a Subject

Say you want to write a *Raiders of the Lost Ark* type of adventure story because you're passionate about Aztecs and Aztec ruins and want to tell the world about this fascinating subject. So you have a main character who's an archaeologist, and because you can't resist sharing your knowledge, you have this character giving frequent impromptu detailed lectures on Aztec history to anyone who will listen. Proceed with caution!

Just drop in a few tantalizing tidbits here and there to pique your readers' interest. If you get them curious enough, they can easily Google Aztecs (or whoever or whatever you're highlighting in your story) and find out a lot more about the topic. You could even add some info at the end of the story somehow, as an Afterword or Glossary or related links or whatever.

~ LENGTHY BACKSTORY ABOUT A CHARACTER

While it is a very good idea to create background information on all of your main characters for yourself, be sure to avoid copying and pasting it into your story in blocks, like a mini-biography or a resume. I've edited novels where a new character comes onto the scene and the writer feels compelled to immediately write a paragraph or three – or even a page or two – of background on that character, to introduce him or her to the readers, for example:

> Kate heard her cell phone ringing. "Excuse me." She grabbed it from her purse and flipped it open. It was her husband Gary.
> Gary, who was forty-two, was an engineer for the city. He and Kate had attended the same college when they were young. Kate

37

was in Nursing and Gary was in Engineering, and they'd met at a dance arranged by the two faculties. They dated through college and married the year after they graduated. By then, Kate was a nurse and Gary was an engineer. They waited a few years before starting a family...[yadda yadda].

"Hi, Gary," Kate said into the phone. "What's up?"

Does the reader need to know all that backstory? Probably not. Certainly not all at once, in the second between the ringing of Kate's phone and when she answers it. Any of it that you feel is necessary can be introduced gradually through dialogue, thoughts, and short exposition.

The problem with filling us in on somebody's background in a paragraph or more like that is that the plot has come to a skidding halt. Secondly, why would we even care about all those little details when that character has just come onstage? Wait until we warm up to them a bit, then provide any pertinent info little by little as we go along.

Also, discovering tidbits about their background as the story progresses mirrors how we get to know people in real life, and also adds interest and intrigue, especially when you drop little hints earlier on, to pique the reader's curiosity.

So it's best to only include what readers really need to know about the character at that point to reveal motivations and drive the plot forward, and continue to marble the info in in small bits as you go along.

Whatever method you choose, make sure the info fits naturally and organically into the conversation, and doesn't look like it's been planted there by the author to get the info across to the readers. Which brings us to our last subtopic:

~ DUMPING INTO DIALOGUE

Don't let your characters lecture or pontificate in dialogue, either. It's just not natural, and will bore the readers just as much as an author aside or intrusion. Avoid "info dumps" in the guise of dialogue – in real life, no one likes to be lectured to in a casual conversation.

Replace long monologues of information with questions and answers or a lively discussion, and keep it relevant to the scene question. And, for more interest, *insert some attitude and tension* in the give-and-take – a little (or a lot) of arguing about facts, or their significance, for example.

~ AYKB – "As you know, Bob…"

This is where the author has one person telling another a bunch of stuff they both know, just to impart that information to the reader. Here's an exaggerated example, to illustrate:

Ralph said to his brother, "As you know, Bob, our parents were both killed in a car crash when we were young, and we were raised by our grandparents."

Readers today are too sophisticated to go for this type of amateurish, heavy-handed information-sharing, and if you do it too often, it's sure to erode their respect and your credibility.

It can even seem a bit "off" when it's more subtle, as when one homicide detective says to another, "Serial killers have usually been abused as children, and their victims often have similarities."

DOING IT RIGHT – Tips for Imparting Info in a Natural Way

~ Add info on a "need to know" basis only.

Don't feel you need to justify all your research or planning by including everything you discovered about a topic or brainstormed about a character's background.

Don't get hung up on adding in every little bit of "fascinating" information just because you went to all that work of researching or inventing it.

But what about info that's essential or relevant to your story? There are ways to slip that in without interrupting the narrative flow or dumping a pile of information on the readers. For example:

~ **A lively question-and-answer dialogue,** where the information is important to one of the characters and maybe the other one is holding back. Don't go on forever, and include some tension. Or someone is picking someone else's brain about something, and the stakes are important.

~ **A character piecing together the facts.** Your viewpoint character has to recall some critical information he or she once knew, and works to remember or find it. Spread this out over pages or chapters, as they gradually find out more.

~ **Detective at work.** Your protagonist is researching critical information on the computer or in the library. Show what she learns as thoughts or in dialogue – but only what is essential for the plotline. And give her emotional reaction to what she's learned, and to how the new info changes things. And again, have her discover facts little by little.

~ **Interviewing.** Your character is questioning various people to solve a problem. Show some of the interview in real time, with dialogue.

~ **On the news.** He's reading the newspaper or watching the news or other TV show, where he learns some new information on a subject. Show how this info is relevant or critical to the problem he's trying to solve.

~ **Brief, vivid flashbacks.** For backstory, use flashbacks and show them in real time, with emotions, action and dialogue. But keep them fairly short. Also, flashbacks need to be emotionally triggered by something that's happening in your story, so they flow naturally out of and back into that point in the story.

So if you need to give your readers some background or essential information, work it in as you go along, in natural, brief, interesting ways, with lots of interaction and some attitude, tension, or out-and-out conflict. And perhaps rethink whether any more detailed information is really needed in your story. Remember, if any readers want to know more, they can always Google the topic. Leave the lectures for the classroom, articles, or nonfiction books – the goal of fiction is to entertain the readers with a riveting story. Period.

Chapter 9 – NEED TO IMPART FACTUAL INFO? USE LOTS OF ATTITUDE!

Strategies for Turning Impersonal Info Dumps into Compelling Copy

As a freelance fiction editor, I find that military personnel, professionals, academics, police officers, and others who are used to imparting factual information in objective, detached, bias-free ways often need a lot of coaching in loosening up their language and adding attitude and emotions to create a captivating story world.

~ Really need those facts in there? Rewrite with attitude!

Say you want to write a fast-paced novel and your background is in a specialized field, so you decide to set your story in that milieu you know so well. Maybe you want to write a legal thriller or a medical suspense, or a mystery involving scientific research or stolen artifacts. Or maybe you'd like to use your military, police, or forensics experience, but your writing experience to date has mainly been confined to producing terse, objective, factual reports.

As you're writing your story, you decide at various points that you need to interrupt the story to explain something the readers may not understand. And you want to get it right, both to lend credibility to your story and because you're concerned about criticism from other professionals in your field. Your first impulse might be to copy and paste sections on that topic from a journal or online search, then tweak them a bit. Or just stop to explain the technical points in your own words, factually, as you would in a report or research paper, then go back to your storyline. Big mistake. You've just interrupted an exciting (we hope!) story to give a mini-lecture. Remember that the main purpose of fiction is to entertain your readers with an engaging tale. To do that, it's critical to stay in the story and in the viewpoint and voice of your compelling, charismatic (we hope!) characters.

~ How to keep your credibility but write with passion and tension

Want to keep your readers turning the pages? Try to turn off possible reactions of colleagues in your field and remind yourself that your goal here is to entertain a broad spectrum of the population with a riveting story. So limit your factual, informative details to only what is necessary for the plot, and present them through the character's point of view, with lots of tension and *attitude*. Go through the section several times and keep loosening up the words and sentence structure to take out the stuffiness and achieve a more casual tone, in the voice of the point of view character for that scene – it needs to be their thoughts, not the author stepping in. And introduce emotions and reactions – make the character frustrated, angry, or anxious.

And if it still sounds like a university lecture or a journal entry, make your character less reserved, less nerdy, less buried in his work. Give him more charisma and universal appeal, even a bad-boy rebellious side, and add quirks and more attitude.

Better yet, insert another, contrasting character to the mix to add in some tension, conflict and contrast.

So to impart some specific information while keeping your readers turning the pages, try these steps:

1. First, in a separate file, copy or write the bare facts in a paragraph or two – up to a page.
2. Go in and loosen up the language a bit – rewrite it in layman's language.
3. Choose two interesting characters who each have some kind of stake in this info and are passionate about the topic, but in different ways.
4. Give them both charisma and quirks – and opposite personalities. Maybe make them competitive or distrustful.
5. Give them each their unique voice, based on their personality differences.
6. Give them opposing views on the topic or conflicting goals.
7. Using those facts, create a question-and-answer or argumentative dialogue between the two characters.

8. Add in some character actions, reactions and sensory details. Now it's starting to read like fiction!

Remember, most of your readers will be outside your field of specialty, and won't find those dry factual details as fascinating as you do!

~ A before-and-after example, disguised from my editing:

Replacing a factual report with a lively dialogue:

Setup: A rebellious, trigger-happy cop has been ordered to be examined by a psychiatrist.

The "info dump" part starts with "Dr. Brown flipped..."

Before:

Dr. Brown opened up Jake's file. "What happened after you were discharged from the Army?"

"I decided to become a cop. After police academy, I was assigned a beat in the Washington Park area in the South Side of Chicago."

"The Washington Park area?" Dr. Brown asked. "That's a pretty rough part of town."

"Yeah, it reminded me of downtown Baghdad," Jake quipped.

Dr. Brown flipped a few pages in the file where there was some background on Washington Park. The summary stated the area was only 1.48 square miles but was usually considered either the most dangerous or second most dangerous neighborhood in the United States. In fact, in some years it had seen more than three hundred violent crimes committed on its turf. Crimes such as murder, robbery, drug-dealing, assaults, prostitution, and rape were committed regularly in Washington Park.

After:

Here, the author has replaced the above factual paragraph with a dialogue.

Dr. Brown opened up Jake's file. "What happened after you

were discharged from the Army?"

"I decided to become a cop. After police academy, I was assigned a beat in Washington Park in South Chicago."

"Washington Park?" Dr. Brown asked. "That's a pretty rough area, I hear."

"Yeah, it reminded me of downtown Baghdad," Jake quipped.

"How so?"

"The area is tiny, barely one and a half square miles, but it's infested with crime. Some years you get more than three hundred violent crimes there."

"Really?"

"Yeah, murder, drug-dealing, robbery, assaults, prostitution, rape—you name it, they're all run-of-the-mill activities in that area. Stress city, man—I made my bones there."

~ How the experts do it – with attitude!

Here are some excerpts from a scene in a crime lab, as an excellent example of how a bestselling thriller author, Robert Crais, reveals the details of the fingerprinting process without interrupting the story to fill in the reader as an author aside:

[...] The white smear was aluminum powder. The brown stains were a chemical called ninhydrin, which reacts with the amino acids left whenever you touch something.

Starkey bent for a closer inspection, then frowned at Chen as if he was stupid.

"This thing's been in the sun for days. It's too old to pick up latents with powder."

"It's also the fastest way to get an image into the system. I figured it was worth the shot."

Starkey grunted. She was okay with whatever might be faster.

"The nin doesn't look much better."

"Too much dust, and the sunlight probably broke down the aminos. I was hoping we'd get lucky with that, but I'm gonna have to glue it."

"Shit. How long?"

I said, "What does that mean, you have to glue it?"

Now Chen looked at me as if I was the one who was stupid. We had a food chain for stupidity going, and I was at the bottom.

"Don't you know what a fingerprint is?"

Starkey said, "He doesn't need a lecture. Just glue the damned thing."

And it goes on like this. Entertaining reading, and we're learning some interesting stuff at the same time.

~ from *The Last Detective*, by Robert Crais

Another good example of how to impart info without boring your readers:

Here's how Lynn Sholes and Joe Moore provide some information on a well-known structure in Las Vegas, without sounding like a travelogue or encyclopedia. This is from *The Blade*, an excellent thriller I edited in late 2012:

Setting: The Strip, Las Vegas

"So the Reverend Hershel Applewhite is a liar," I said when Kenny returned from accompanying Carl down to the hotel lobby.

I stood at the window staring at the imposing pyramid-shaped Alexandria Hotel in the distance. I'd read somewhere that the forty-two-billion candlepower spotlight at the top of the hotel could be seen from space. The same guy who designed it—I couldn't remember his name—built similar pyramid hotels with beacons in South Africa and China. Claimed he wanted his lights to be seen from every corner of the world.

Chapter 10 – WRITING TENSE ACTION SCENES

I specialize in editing thrillers, and I sometimes get asked how editing suspense fiction is different from editing other genres. That's a huge topic, too long for only one chapter, and would include specific approaches to various elements like premise, plot, characterization, pacing, word choice, and writing style. For this chapter, I'll just talk about writing effective action scenes, which can appear in many other genres besides thrillers.

When your characters are running for their lives, or your hero is in a race against time to save innocent lives, it's time to write tight and leave out a lot of description, especially little insignificant details about their surroundings. Characters on the run don't have time to admire the scenery or décor, start musing about a moment in the past, or have great long thoughts or discussions. Their adrenaline is pumping and all they're thinking of is survival – theirs and/or someone else's.

Of course, if the details of the setting are significant or would somehow help or hinder your protagonist, then definitely include them. Basically, put yourself in the head and body of your character under stress, fighting for her life, and see/hear/smell/feel what she does, then react as she reacts.

SOME QUICK TIPS FOR WRITING STRONG ACTION SCENES

~ **Show, don't tell** (of course!).
Play the scene in real time, with actions, reactions, and dialogue.

~ **Use deep point of view.**
Stay in the POV (point of view) character's head and body.

46

~ Avoid info dumps.
Keep the readers right there in the scene with the characters. Don't intrude as the author to clarify anything. If details need explaining, fit that in somehow before the tense scene starts.

~ Evoke the senses.
Show your viewpoint character's vivid sensory impressions, so the reader sees, hears, smells, tastes, feels what he does.

~ Amp up the imagery.
Use the most concrete, suggestive nouns and the most powerful, evocative verbs you can find.

~ Show inner reactions.
Reveal your POV character's emotions, brief thoughts, and physical reactions, starting with their visceral responses.

~ Use tight, staccato thinking.
Avoid long, involved thought processes, which deflate tension and slow things down.

~ Describe physical actions succinctly, for fast pacing and high tension.
Don't get into distracting minor details about which hand or finger or foot and exactly how high or low, unless it's important for some reason.

~ Show other characters' threats and reactions.
Do this through their words, tone of voice, actions, body language, and facial expressions.

~ Use rapid-fire dialogue.
Avoid complete, correct, thoughtful sentences and lengthy discussions among characters.

~ Write tight.
Cut out any little unneeded words that are cluttering up sentences and slowing down the pace.

~ Use short sentences and paragraphs,
for a tense, breathless, staccato effect.

SOME BEFORE-AND-AFTER EXAMPLES OF
EFFECTIVE ACTION SCENES

(Well-disguised from my editing. The "after" examples are of course only one possibility among many.)

Before:

Fortunately for Jennifer, the attacker was far enough away that when he attempted to grab her she sidestepped him and delivered a sharp kick to the outside of his left knee.

He grunted and fell back against the stack of wooden crates. He then got up clumsily, rubbing his arm, showing his anger at how easily Jennifer had dodged and hit him.

After:

The attacker lunged at Jennifer. She dodged to the side and delivered a sharp kick to his knee.

He grunted and fell against the stack of wooden crates. He scrambled up, rubbing his arm, eyes full of hate.

Before:

His facial expression changed from one showing loathing to one communicating unrestrained cunning and anticipation. Jennifer realized at that moment that she had made a fatal mistake. She looked to her right. The door leading out of the warehouse was about fifty feet from where she was standing.

After:

His expression changed from loathing to wily anticipation. Jennifer knew she had made a fatal mistake. She searched for the exit door. It was to her right, about fifty feet away.

Before:

Kate and Lauren ran down the tunnel to an open doorway, then up some stone steps leading to a stone walkway. Kate hesitated for only a moment at the top in order to jam the hand gun she was holding into her waistband and give her time to figure out where to run.

In front of them was a huge stone courtyard, which was too

open for them to safely cross before the smugglers would come looking for them. Kate knew she had to find a hiding place quickly. Then it came to her.

"Follow me," Kate commanded, running off to her left.

"Where are we going?" Lauren asked, as she ran beside Kate.

"To the ancient pavilion. It's halfway down the east wall of the courtyard. From there, we can access other parts of the ruins if we need to escape from the men who I know will soon be looking for us."

[First paragraph has too much minor, unnecessary detail. In the last paragraph, her language is too correct and formal, especially for someone out of breath and running for her life! And all that detail isn't necessary, as she'll be leading the way, anyway.]

After:

Kate and Lauren sprinted down the tunnel, then up some stone steps to a walkway. At the top, Kate stopped to jam the gun into her waistband and figure out where to run.

In front of them was a wide open stone courtyard. They'd never get across without the smugglers spotting them. Kate knew she had to find a hiding place quickly. Then it came to her.

"Follow me," Kate said, dashing off to her left.

"Where are we going?" Lauren asked as she raced to keep up.

"To the pavilion. We can hide in the ruins behind it."

See "You Be the Editor" near the end of the book for passages to try to make tighter and tenser.

Chapter 11 – VOICE: THAT ELUSIVE BUT CRITICAL INGREDIENT OF COMPELLING FICTION

Voice – what is it exactly?

Literary agents and acquiring editors always say they're looking for fiction with a compelling, unique, fresh, natural voice. Then when asked to define it, they hem and haw a bit, searching for the right words to try to capture what they mean by a voice that appeals to readers and makes them want to keep reading.

From what I've gathered from my varied reading and workshops, the ideal "voice" is that natural, open, appealing, charismatic tone and style that draws us in and makes us feel like we know the characters well – and want to get to know them better!

HOW CAN WE DEVELOP AN APPEALING VOICE?

These tips, a mix of advice from others and my own ideas, will be helpful to writers who are still in the process of finding their voice or fine-tuning it to make it more relaxed, powerful and appealing.

~ Don't lecture your readers.

As Bruce DeSilva said in his workshop on this topic at Craftfest / Thrillerfest 2012 in New York, many aspiring authors need to first free themselves from the constraints of their more formal, correct writing background, especially if it includes graduate degrees and a lot of legal, academic or business writing. So shake yourself loose of all those constraints and find your more casual, accessible, appealing inner voice. How do you do that?

~ Write in a clear, direct way.

Forget all those long, convoluted sentences and pretentious words and learn to write in a clear, direct, accessible, casual style that evokes the senses and appeals to the emotions. Streamline your writing!

~ Write to one person.

To help develop an intimacy with your readership and a conversational tone, create or choose one single person you're writing to, who is warm, friendly, open to your ideas, interested, and intelligent.

DeSilva suggests choosing a close friend or family member to write to, but personally, I advise against writing to someone in your inner circle, as you might end up skipping over a lot of details and points that need to be there for other readers who don't share your background, cultural environment, and basic frames of reference.

So I suggest creating an ideal reader. Write a brief description of their age, gender, background, home and work situation, personality, and interests (which of course include reading your kind of writing!). Get to know them a bit by giving them some positive attributes that will help you feel comfortable and open with them. Then target your writing to this person. Relax and let the real you come through.

~ Read and imitate writers whose voice you really enjoy.

Don't copy their words verbatim, of course, but immerse yourself in their story world, told in their unique voice. Read their books aloud to really internalize the rhythm of their language, the phrasing and expressions and word choices that appeal to you so much. Then of course adapt the cadence and rhythm and attitudes and vocabulary to your own situation.

~ Write a chapter in first person, then change it to third person.

One author whose voice I love is Janet Evanovich, whose spunky, quirky heroine, Stephanie Plum, narrates her story in first-person point of view. But it's hard to write first-person well, and it can be limiting, as you're confined to scenes where this character is present. Also, first-person isn't always the best choice for, say, a thriller, as you want other viewpoints in there, too, notably that of the antagonist.

But try writing several pages or a chapter or two in first-person ("I"), to develop your main character's unique voice, then just go back and rewrite them in third person (he/she), with as few other changes as possible.

~ Read your story out loud to test its authenticity and easy flow.

As DeSilva says, your writing should have the rhythm and comfortable familiarity of spoken language. If it doesn't flow easily, go in and streamline the language to take out the convoluted sentences, clunky phrasing, and fancy-shmancy words. Or hire a trusted writer friend or reputable freelance editor to go through it for you to take out anything that sounds too formal, wordy, or erudite.

~ Write in deep point of view or close third.

This means the story is unfolding mainly through the thoughts and reactions and emotions and attitudes of your protagonist. Even descriptions of your setting should be filtered through your protagonist's (or other viewpoint character's) preferences, views, and mood. This ensures that your whole novel has a great, unique voice, not just the dialogue. See my blog posts, POV 101, POV 102 & POV 103, on *The Writer's Forensics Blog*.

~ Give each character his or her own voice.

When you're writing dialogue, each character should sound different, with their own unique speech patterns, word choices, and slang or pet expressions, based on their milieu, upbringing, education, and personality. Listen in on all kinds of conversations, both in real life and on TV and in movies.

Develop an ear for how different people speak. To improve the idiosyncratic speech of a character in your novel, try journaling in their voice, in first person. Just write freely, using lots of attitude! Eventually, you'll get into their rhythm and find the words that seem to suit them best.

So break free from the constraints of your background, education, and any more formal work-related writing, and write the story only you can write, with your unique experiences and personality, in your own direct, open, interesting voice. Don't hold back – relax and reveal yourself.

Part II

Write Tight

Chapter 12 – HOW TO SLASH YOUR WORD COUNT BY 20-50%

...and tighten up your story without losing any of the good stuff!

Have you been told your story looks promising or even intriguing, but your novel is way too long? Today's readers have shorter attention spans, and publishers don't want to accept long novels from new writers, as they are so much more expensive to produce.

The current preferred length for thrillers, mysteries and romance is around 70,000–90,000 words. Anything over100 thousand words is definitely considered too long in most genres these days. Well-written, finely crafted fantasies and historical sagas can run longer, but newbie writers need to earn their stripes first before attempting to sell a really long novel. Basically, every word needs to count. Every image and decision and action and reaction needs to drive the story forward. There's no place for rambling or waxing eloquent or self-indulgent preening in today's popular fiction! Thrillers and other suspense novels especially need to be fast-paced page-turners.

A STEP-BY-STEP STRATEGY FOR CUTTING THE WORD COUNT

It's best to proceed roughly in this order, using any strategies that apply to your novel:

START WITH BIG CHANGES TO PLOT, CHARACTERS, AND STRUCTURE:

~ Divide into two or three books?

If you have an intricate, involved plot, can you divide your really long novel into two or three in a series? Bear in mind, though, that each book in the series needs its own plot arc and character arc – rising tension and some resolution, and a change/growth in the protagonist.

~ Condense an overly long, involved plot.

If the story doesn't lend itself to being broken up, try making your plot less detailed. Cut or combine some of your less exciting plot points. Cut down on some of the "and then, and then, and then…"

~ Too many subplots?

Delete one or two (or three) subplots, depending on how many you have.

~ Cut back on your cast of thousands.

Too many characters can be confusing and annoying to the readers. Find places where you can combine two or three characters into one. And don't get into involved descriptions of minor, walk-on characters.

~ Start later.

Consider deleting or condensing chapter one. Maybe even chapter two, too. Take out the warm-up, where you're revving your engine, and start your story later.

~ Reduce backstory.

Take out all or almost all background info (character history) in the first few chapters and marble in just the essentials as you go along, on an "as-needed" basis only. This also helps add intrigue.

~ Cut out some chapters.

Delete most or all of any chapters that don't have enough tension and change, that don't drive the story forward. Add any essential bits to other chapters. (Save deleted stuff on another file.) Or condense two chapters and combine them into one.

~ Cut out some scenes.

Delete or condense scenes that don't have enough tension or change, or add much to the plot or characterization. Condense parts where scenes drag, eliminating the boring bits. (Take out the parts that readers skip over.) See Chapter 10.

~ Take out any weak links.

Also, remnants from earlier versions and anything that just doesn't fit there anymore (if it ever did).

THEN EVALUATE YOUR WRITING STYLE AND THE INTERNAL STRUCTURE OF YOUR CHAPTERS AND SCENES:

~ Cut back on rambling or overly detailed descriptions.

With today's access to TV, movies, the internet and travel, we no longer need the kind of detail readers of 100 years ago needed to understand the setting, so just paint with broad brush strokes and leave out all the little details. Also, don't describe the setting in neutral language. Filter any descriptions of surroundings through the eyes, ears, and attitude of your point of view character.

~ Same with characters – no need to go into great detail.

Give the most obvious and interesting details, and let the readers fill in the rest to their heart's content.

~ Take out summaries or detailed references to scenes we've already seen.

Don't have a character relating the details to another character of something that happened that the readers witnessed first-hand and already know about. Skip over it with a phrase like "She told him how she'd gotten injured."

~ Start scenes and chapters later and end them sooner.

Cut out the warm-up and cool-down.

~ Skip over transitional times when not much happens.

Replace with one or two sentences, like "Three days later,".

~ Eliminate or severely condense any "explanations" on topics or people.

Keep these to the bare minimum, and give the info from a character's point of view, with attitude, or through a lively conversation or heated argument. See Chapters 8 and 9.

~ Delete or condense info dumps.

Take out any long explanations, self-indulgent rambling on pet topics, "teaching" sections, or rants. See Chapters 8 and 9.

~ Eliminate repetitions and redundancies.

Just say it once – no need to say it again in a different way. You may think that will help emphasize your point, but it actually has the opposite effect. For more detail on this, see Chapters 13, 14 & 15.

FINALLY, TIGHTEN YOUR WRITING TO CREATE LEANER PARAGRAPHS AND SENTENCES:

~ Take out one of each:

Try to delete one paragraph per page (or two); one sentence (or more) in each paragraph, and at least one word, preferably more, in each sentence. Cut out the deadwood!

~ Cut the clutter and cut to the chase.

Do a search for all those unnecessary words that are just taking up space or weakening your prose, and delete most of them. See Chapters 14 & 15.

Chapter 13 – DON'T INSULT YOUR READERS
BY OVEREXPLAINING

If you want to write compelling fiction that sells (and who doesn't?), when you're revising, keep an eye (and ear) out for those boring, repetitive sentences and passages and delete them. Resist the urge to explain a point to your readers or say the same thing several different ways, just to be sure they got it.

If you "show" a character's feelings (as is most powerful and immediate), no need to follow that up by "telling" readers how they felt, too. That's overkill and comes across as patronizing. Today's readers are sophisticated and savvy, so make your point, then move on.

Sure, go ahead and write more leisurely the first time through, exploring different ways to express various ideas or to show character reactions or motivations. But then later, save the doc in a new file and get out your red pen or hover your finger over your "Delete" key and start taking out all those "supporting phrases" that pile up and actually dilute the power of a single phrase or image that stands alone.

ONE PLUS ONE EQUALS A HALF

Whether you're trying to set a mood with imagery, deepen characterization, or advance the plot with action or dialogue, it's best to just say/show/describe it once – twice maximum – not three or four times. Believe it or not, if you keep saying the same thing over and over, even if it's in a variety of ways, the end result will be less, not more. This is what Sol Stein calls "One plus one equals a half" in his chapter, "Liposuctioning Flab."

You may think you're emphasizing something by repeating it, but even if you say it in different words, you clutter up the sentence or paragraph, and the overall impact is diminished, reducing it to half of the impact it would have had with just one of the images or sentences.

A lot of my editing consists of finding these "one plus ones" (or "plus twos" or more), and helping the authors eliminate or reduce the weaker repetitions of ideas.

Here's an example, well-disguised from my editing, of saying basically the same thing three or four or five times within a paragraph.

Before:
> Enraged by the CEO's false accusations, Cheryl struggled to regain control of her emotions. She didn't often lose her temper but when it happened, she found it difficult to calm down. She had never been so angry at any time in her professional career. Mr. Johnson had pushed her too far when he suggested that she could possibly be involved in stealing those confidential documents. Just thinking about what he said made her blood boil.

After:
> Enraged by the CEO's false accusations, Cheryl struggled to regain control of her emotions. How dare he suggest that she could be involved in stealing those confidential documents? Just thinking about it made her blood boil.

Paring the ideas in the "Before" paragraph down to the essentials increases the power of the message. Repeating it several times actually detracts from the message and dilutes it.

Here's another one:

Before:
> *If I hadn't told Ellen to leave, she might still be alive.* Anne knew the guilt she was feeling at not being there for Ellen would forever torment her. She wasn't sure she could ever forgive herself.

The last sentence above can be deleted as it's redundant, and the one before it will have more power when it stands alone, and ends the paragraph:

After:

> *If I hadn't told Ellen to leave, she might still be alive.* Anne knew the guilt she was feeling at not being there for Ellen would forever torment her.

Often less is more, in the sense of having more impact, whereas if you overexplain or repeat the idea/message, it dilutes the power and impact of the statement.

RUE: RESIST THE URGE TO EXPLAIN

"Resist the Urge to Explain" was coined by Renni Browne and Dave King in their book, *Self-Editing for Fiction Writers*. Basically, it's about honing your fiction-writing skills so your dialogue, actions, and evocation of characters' inner feelings and reactions come to life on the page. Resist the urge to add some clarifications afterward to explain what you meant.

~ Don't restate the obvious – the readers get it!

If your POV character is trying to mislead another character, or being sarcastic or evasive, write it in such a way that the reader, who is in that character's head, is able to read between the lines and understand that his words are covering up his real intentions. Don't add a sentence or two at the end to explain to the reader that he was bluffing or lying or manipulating! That's insulting to the reader, who has just been feeling clever along with your MC, about successfully fooling someone. If you spell it out, the reader will feel patronized.

In a scene from my editing, which I have altered considerably to protect the author, a con-artist is trying to open a bank account with a large bag of cash. The banker hesitates, so the con-man threatens to take his business elsewhere. He gets up and is about to leave when the banker relents and tells him it's okay.

After showing us by his inner thoughts that the bad guy was just bluffing to manipulate the situation, the writer adds at the end, "Griff acted reluctant as he sat back down. In reality he had no intention of leaving. He just wanted the banker to think he did."

Those last two sentences are condescending to the reader. Don't elaborate on characters' motivations for doing something. That can come across as clumsy or too obvious – not to mention insulting.

The above example is an obvious one, but even saying the same thing two or three times in slightly different ways can be overkill and can make a reader want to shout, "Okay, okay! Enough already! I got it the first time!"

~ Show, Don't Tell

Show us how the character is feeling or reacting. Then resist the urge to explain (tell) it afterward, just to be sure the reader got it:

"Finally! I was wondering when you'd call back. Where the hell have you been? You'll never believe what happened!" Jason's voice was brimming with emotion, overexcited.

Jason's words say it all, so no need to tell us how his voice sounds. In a situation where Jason is actually present and not on the phone, you could use an action beat, like, "Jason's eyes were wide and he was bouncing on his toes," or whatever.

Or another overly wordy example:

"Perhaps you're right," he conceded, an inflection of doubt creeping into his voice.

Why not just leave it at:

"Perhaps you're right," he said.

Or again, add an action beat after it.

This tendency to overexplain can show up in minor ways that are just as indicative of amateurish writing, like the examples below, where the last sentence in each is superfluous and should be taken out.

"You idiot!" she yelled, throwing the picture across the room. She was furious.

"I wish Daddy would come home. I miss him." The little girl was sad.

In each instance, the second sentence is not only unnecessary; it detracts from the message of the first, and is a bit patronizing to the reader, who got it from the initial sentences. Also, the first sentence *shows* and the second sentence *tells*. When you explain emotions and reactions to the reader, it's as if you're covering your tracks, in case your initial description or dialogue didn't show it well enough.

So resist the urge to describe (tell) how your character feels. Instead, dramatize (show) it for the reader with precise words and strong imagery.

Same thing with phrases like, "he/she (verb) (-ly adverb)."

Instead of:

"That's my girl!" Dad said proudly, smiling and patting her on the back.

Say:

"That's my girl!" Dad smiled and patted her on the back.

No need to say "said proudly." What they say plus their actions or inner reactions should make it clear how they're feeling. Don't explain to the reader after the fact. And again, that's telling. Take most of those -ly adverbs out and show what's going on, both physically and emotionally, by the actions, dialogue, and inner reactions and thoughts.

~ Don't retell readers what they already know from what you've said, for example:

"We will find out who you are. We have eyes and ears everywhere. You are not safe from us." The cold tone and intimidating words underlined the obvious menace of the caller.

What follows the quoted words is overexplaining, which can make readers feel like you're talking down to them.

~ Subtle is more sophisticated.

Rather than stating the obvious, it's more powerful to hint at it. It's often best not to spell it out, especially if it has to do with a character's inner thoughts or suppressed feelings. Subtext leaves the readers with more satisfaction that they're successfully reading between the lines.

As Jessica Page Morrell says so eloquently in her excellent craft of writing book, *Between the Lines*,

> "Find ways to insert subtext – the unspoken, the innuendo, the nuanced moments that are not directly represented, and the actions that speak of feelings that are too volatile to express out loud. Also, look for times in your story to pull back, to allow the reader to bring her own understanding of human nature into your story."

So be on the lookout for places where you may be inadvertently patronizing your reader by overstating things.

Resources:
Jodie's editing, and
Renni Browne and Dave King, *Self-Editing for Fiction Writers*
Jessica Page Morrell, *Between the Lines*
Sol Stein, *Stein on Writing*

Chapter 14 – SHED THOSE WORDY HABITS
AND CUT TO THE CHASE

Aspiring fiction writers often need help with kicking bad writing habits, like overly long, convoluted or just clunky sentences; weak, lackluster word choices; clichéd imagery; and belabored points. Newbie writers often have a tendency to repeat words, phrasing, ideas or imagery to emphasize their point, which actually diminishes the impact of the passage.

CUT THE CLUTTER AND STREAMLINE
YOUR WRITING

In editing fiction manuscripts, one of my most important jobs is to help authors streamline their writing so the ideas flow more smoothly. I'm talking about finding and slashing those extra words that aren't needed to enhance the mood, plot or characterization, or bring the story to life; the clutter of words that are getting in the way of the imagery and story and slowing down the pace.

Think of a flower garden that is stifled by weeds to the point where you can't see the flowers. Or a cluttered basement or workshop, where you can't find the things you really need. The good stuff gets lost, or at least difficult to find among all the junk.

~ Go for flow.

So once you've gotten through your first draft and made sure every chapter and scene is pulling its weight in terms of content, it's important to go back in and start again, looking for wordiness and redundancies to cut ruthlessly in order to make your ideas flow better, pick up the pace, and increase the tension and sense of urgency, so readers can't stop turning the pages.

But of course, I won't be advising you to cut so drastically that you take out all the great imagery and emotions. No need to make your style so laconic that you've sucked the life and voice out of it. Keep all those juicy words and phrases that set the tone, define your voice and attitude, add atmosphere, provide sensory details, deepen your characters, add to the suspense and intrigue, and so on. Just cut out the excess blah-blah and leave the gems behind.

~ Liposuction that fat.

Sol Stein calls this important part of the editorial process "liposuctioning the flab." As he says, "Flab is the enemy of every writer. Superfluous words and phrases soften prose. […] Flab, if not removed, can have a deleterious effect on the impatient reader, who will pay less attention to each word and begin to skip…." And after you go through and cut the flab, the remaining text will be much stronger and more compelling.

So if you want your fiction to sell, here's some clutter to look for and expel, so the readers have nothing between them and your story.

QUICK TIPS WITH EXAMPLES FOR DECLUTTERING YOUR SENTENCES

~ Take out empty, filler words like "It was," "there was," and "there were."*

*Unless you're bestselling author Lee Child, who ignores this and a lot of other fiction-writing advice! When you're as good a storyteller and as successful as Child, you can write your own rules, too.

Some disguised examples from my editing:

Before:
>   I headed down a rickety set of wooden steps to the basement. **There was** a dim light ahead in the hallway. To the right **there were** cardboard boxes stacked high. To the left, **there was** a closed door with a padlock. Suddenly, I heard muffled sounds. **There was** someone upstairs.

Cut to the Chase

After:
>I headed down a rickety set of wooden steps to the dimly lit basement. To the right cardboard boxes were stacked high. To the left, I saw a closed door with a padlock. Suddenly, I heard muffled sounds. Someone was upstairs.

I could play around with this some more, but you get the picture.

~ Take out the word "that" wherever it's not needed.

Read the sentence out loud, and if it still makes sense without the "that," remove it. Smooths out the sentence, so it's less clunky and flows better.

Not: He told me **that** he'd be here at five.

But: He told me he'd be here at five.

Not: The dog **that** you gave me is growing fast.

But: The dog you gave me is growing fast.

Before:
>She said **that** you thought **that** it was too expensive and **that** you wanted to shop around.

After:
>She said you thought it was too expensive and you wanted to shop around.

However, be sure to keep the "that" if it's necessary for meaning, or if omitting it will cause even momentary confusion and force the reader to read the sentence again.

For example:

>Norris knew all the guys on the SWAT team preparing to storm the building were familiar with the layout of every floor.

This sentence would first be read as "Norris knew all the guys on the SWAT team," which would cause momentary confusion, then the reader would have to readjust their thinking. So best to keep the "that" in this passage:

> Norris knew that all the guys on the SWAT team preparing to storm the building were familiar with the layout of every floor.

Or:
> Maybe a one-on-one with her would make her see things differently. Surely she would see the girls were in danger.

In the example above, the reader first reads "Surely she would see the girls." So it's better to leave the "that" in there to avoid confusion:

> Maybe a one-on-one with her would make her see things differently. Surely she would see that the girls were in danger.

~ Take out unneeded dialogue tags.

Remove "he said" or "she said" where it's obvious who's speaking. But don't take them all out – that can be annoying if the reader is forced to check back four or five lines to see who's talking now. A good trick is to replace the "he/she said" with an action beat:

Before:
> He opened the curtains **and said**, "It's a beautiful day."

After:
> He opened the curtains. "It's a beautiful day."

Before:
> "Want some more coffee?" **she said, pointing** to his empty mug.

After:
> "Want some more coffee?" **She pointed** to his empty mug.

Or:
> "I'll be right back." He ran out the door.

No need to say: he said, running out the door.

MANAGE THOSE MODIFIERS

~ **Banish those wishy-washy qualifiers.**

Find and take out almost all of your qualifiers like *quite, rather, often, somewhat, kind of, mildly, a bit, mostly, usually, pretty, a little, mainly, generally, basically, almost,* and *sort of,* which just dilute your message, weaken the imagery, and dissipate the tension. Start by doing a "Find and Replace" for the words "very" and "quite" and just take them all out.

Before:
   "I'm **honestly quite** surprised and **a bit** disappointed at her reaction, as I **kind of** thought we'd resolved that issue."

After:
   "I'm surprised and disappointed at her reaction, as I thought we'd resolved that issue."

Before:
   She was **rather** worried about the situation, and it was making her **very** tense.

After:
   She was worried about the situation and it was making her tense.

You can see that by taking out the qualifiers, we've strengthened the sentences.

   Jane furtively grabbed hold of her friend's arm, **a mild desperation** suddenly taking control of her mind.

How can you have a mild desperation? This type of writing shows timidity on the part of the author, like, "I'm not sure if I should make her desperate or not." Take a stand – be confident. Go ahead, make your character desperate!

~ **Watch those intensifiers, too.**

Intensifiers like *very, really, extremely, totally, so, too, perfectly, absolutely, completely, truly, particularly,* and *actually* are a lazy way of expressing something. It's quicker and easier to put one of these intensifiers in front of an everyday noun or verb than to search for a more powerful, more descriptive word.

Replace the intensifier plus the word it modifies with stronger, more precise nouns or verbs. (Of course, ignore this for dialogue, especially for *totally awesome* YA fiction!)

Instead of *really cold,* use *freezing* or *frigid* or *icy.* Replace *extremely happy* with *radiant* or *ecstatic* or *blissful* or *delighted* or *exultant.* Rather than, "The very weak old man," say "The frail old man." Instead of "He was very funny," say "He was hilarious." Rather than "We were so hungry," say "We were ravenous."

Instead of *particularly difficult* or *truly tiring,* say *grueling* or *arduous* or *demanding* or *strenuous* or *laborious* or *exhausting* or *backbreaking.* (Again, check your online thesaurus or invest in a really good print one.)

~ Cut way back on adjectives and adverbs.

Many or even most adjectives and adverbs are dispensable. Instead, use your thesaurus to **find stronger, evocative verbs and nouns**. Sol Stein recommends a bold approach: "The quickest way of increasing the pace of a manuscript and strengthening it at the same time is to remove all adjectives and adverbs, and then readmit the necessary few after careful testing."

~ Eliminate most adverbs.

See how many -ly adverbs you can cut. Use a more powerful, more specific verb instead. Rather than "He walked purposefully across the room," say "He strode across the room." Rather than, "he ran quickly," say, "he raced" or "he dashed" or "he sprinted" or "he darted" or "he scurried."

If the verb expresses the action well, delete the adverb after it. No need to write, "She screamed loudly." A scream is loud, so take out "loudly." Same with "He hurriedly scribbled a note." Scribbling implies writing quickly, so the adverb is redundant. Same with "She whispered softly."

~ Find and delete almost all instances of *suddenly* and *immediately*.

Not:
> We were walking along when suddenly a car pulled up beside us.

Just say the car pulled up – no need for "suddenly."

Not:
> He heard a loud noise outside and immediately ran out to see what it was.

We know he did it immediately, so no need to say so.

~ Cut back on adjectives, too.

Then see how many adjectives you can cut. If you describe someone or something with three or four adjectives, can you cut out one or two, and just leave the strongest, most apt one or two? That way, what's left will stand out more and have more power.

Before:
> A beautiful, huge, historic Victorian mansion stood at the top of the hill.

After:
> A beautiful Victorian mansion stood at the top of the hill.

Or:
> A stately Victorian mansion stood at the top of the hill.

~ But keep the gems.

Don't go to extremes and delete all adjectives and adverbs. Some adjectives and adverbs enhance rather than detracting. Here are some tips for deciding which adverbs and adjectives to cut, and which to keep (adapted from advice by Sol Stein).

Keep any adjectives and adverbs that:

- Supply necessary information for reader understanding.
"It's one a.m. Where is she?" she asked frantically.

- Help the reader visualize the precise image or feeling you want to project, for example,
"The out-of-control rollerblader careened wildly down the hill."

- Stimulate the reader's curiosity and keep the story moving along, like:
"She had a haunted look."

SMOOTH OUT CLUNKY, CLUTTERED PHRASING

Examples: Here are some examples from my editing of taking out unnecessary words for better flow. As always, I've changed the names and details to provide anonymity for the writers.

Before:
> As soon as Chris started to rise, Nathan saw it as an indication he was going to follow, and started off back in the direction of the elevator, this time worrying less about his silence and more about haste.

After:
> As soon as Chris started to rise, Nathan turned and hurried toward the elevator.

Before:
> They slept each night in the cheap motels **located less than a mile's drive from the** interstate.

After:
> They slept each night in cheap motels **just off** the interstate.

Before:
> The car drove slowly through the large complex **heading in the direction of** a secluded building **at the back of the facility.**

It was located on the shore of the Mississippi River. The vehicle **came to a stop** next to the entrance **to the building**.

After:

The car drove slowly through the large complex toward a secluded building on the shore of the Mississippi River. It stopped next to the entrance.

Before:

Jordan pulled **the jeep off by the side of the road** by the path to the old cabin.

After:

Jordan pulled **off** by the path to the old cabin.

We know he's driving a jeep on a road, and if he's pulling off the road, it's to the side of it.

Before:

He was shooting off his mouth in the bar last night **telling everybody that he was going to** find the bastard that ratted on him.

After:

He was shooting off his mouth in the bar last night **about** finding the bastard that ratted on him.

Before:

He **moved his mouse pointer over to** the other email **that** he had received.

After:

He **clicked on** the other email he had received.

Or just:

He clicked on the second email.

Chapter 15 – CONDENSE CLUSTERS OF WORDS AND REJECT REPETITIVE REDUNDANCIES

Take out words that restate what is obvious by the rest of the sentence, words that repeat what you've already said, words that are just adding clutter to your sentence.

CONDENSE CLUSTERS OF WORDS

~ Avoid those "little-word pile-ups":

Cluttering your sentences with too many unnecessary words can get in the way of clear communication and confuse and subliminally irritate the reader. Go through your manuscript and see where you've cluttered up sentences and paragraphs with little words and phrases that aren't needed and impede the natural flow of ideas.

Here a few examples of this "little word pile-up" tendency (thanks to Jessica Morrell for this great phrase). Replace the cluttered phrase with a single word, for better flow.

Instead of three or four words => Use one or two

in spite of the fact that => although

as a result of => because

came in contact with => met

at this point in time => now

during the time that => while

he is a man who => he

make use of => use

with reference to => about

in the vicinity of => near

in the direction of => to, at, toward

located at => at

as a consequence of => because

for the simple reason that => because

owing to the fact that => because

a large percentage of => many

has the appearance of => looks like

with the exception of => except for

take into consideration => consider

be in possession of => have

REJECT REPETITIVE REDUNDANCIES

Maybe in an attempt to be very clear, we often fall into the bad habit of using two words together that mean the "exact same" thing, like "repetitive redundancy." It's always best to choose the most precise word and ditch the one that's shoring it up – it's stronger on its own.

~ Replace the repetitive phrase with its concise equivalent:

basic fundamentals => fundamentals

honest truth => truth

future plans => plans

regular routine => routine

past history => history

final outcome => outcome

extremely unique => unique

totally unanimous => unanimous

sudden impulse => impulse

unexpected surprise => surprise

overused cliché => cliché

What's the problem? It's obvious – the only kind of truth is honest truth, an impulse is sudden, repeat means to do something again, a surprise is by nature unexpected, and so on.

~ Delete phrases that reinforce what's already been said.

The phrases in italics are redundant here:

> We passed an abandoned house *that nobody lived in* on a deserted street *with no one around*. The house was gray *in color*.

> At this *point in* time, *the truth is that* complaints are increasing *in number*, but I don't see that as a problem *to be solved*.

~ Avoid repeating the same or similar words or phrases within a few sentences or paragraphs.

A couple of extreme examples of this that I just made up:

> She was **happily** calling all her friends with the **happy** news.

She'd been **unhappy** for so long she wasn't sure she could even trust **happiness** any more.

I had to have someone who could **help** me find the program and Ken wasn't very **helpful**. Whining about it wasn't **helping** either.

And some examples from my editing:

He entered, holding out his **security** pass for the **security** guard at the desk, who nodded and gestured for him to continue.

This would be a hard place for vulnerable **people** like Beatrice Cook, frail old **people**, the single mothers, and mentally challenged **people**.

Shane had everything. A great job. A marriage to a wonderful girl **who** loved him for **who** he was rather than what he had **made him feel** complete. The son she gave birth to **made him feel** on top of the world.

~ Watch for those pet words or phrases you love to use, too.

Do you have characters *gazing* or *sighing* or *stomping* a lot? Do you have a lot of *heaving chests* or *rolling eyes* or *pounding heartbeats* or *clacking heels*? A few of these here and there are fine, of course, but don't overdo it. Often it takes a second set of eyes to notice favorite overused words or phrases of ours that keep showing up. The "Find and Replace" tool is great for this, too.

Resources:
Jodie's editing, and
Robert W. Harris, *When Good People Write Bad Sentences*
Jessica Page Morrell, *Thanks, But This Isn't For Us*
Sol Stein, *Stein on Writing*

Chapter 16 – BREAK THOSE FORMAL OR VERBOSE WRITING HABITS

I've received fiction manuscripts from lots of professionals – several lawyers, several physicians, a university professor, a psychiatrist, several grad students, and a judge – and for many of these clients, my editing often focuses on helping them relax their overly correct writing style. It can be especially challenging for professionals who like the idea of writing a novel but don't have a lot of time to read fiction because of all the work-related reading they have to do.

Writing fiction that sizzles is a world away from nonfiction writing, especially scholarly, professional, or technical copy. In fact, people who have had a lot of experience writing academic, professional, legal, or business documents often have the steepest learning curve when it comes to switching to fiction. Professionals typically have the most "bad habits" to unlearn when they're trying to create a believable story world with a casual, even quirky voice; lively, fast-paced writing; and colorful characters from various walks of life.

To loosen up, read lots of popular fiction.

An excellent first step to counteract stiff, overly correct, nonfiction-type writing habits is to read a lot of bestselling fiction in the genre you want to write. In fact, try reading it aloud, or buy the audio books and listen to them in your car or while puttering around the house or garage. You'll soon get into the rhythm of the writing and start to develop your own natural, compelling fiction voice.

AVOID OVERLY CORRECT, CONVOLUTED SENTENCES

Remember, it's about communicating images and concepts, and carrying your reader along with the story. Don't muddle your message with a lot of extra words that just clutter up the sentence and hamper the free flow of ideas.

Here are some more disguised examples from my fiction editing of trimming excess words:

Before:
"Bastards. Why am I always the last to know?" Pivoting, the detective **walked in the direction of the station's** front desk **with a purposeful, nearly aggressive, gait.** He **shoved himself bodily** through the swinging door and **locked eye contact with** the uniformed officer on reception duty.

After:
"Bastards. Why am I always the last to know?" Pivoting, the detective **marched toward** the front desk. He **slammed** through the swinging door and **glared** at the officer on reception duty.

Before:
Craig paused **a moment before replying as** he slowed the car **in preparation for** a right-hand turn onto a smaller road, **resuming the conversation as** the car **again** picked up speed.

After:
Craig paused **as** he slowed the car **to** turn right onto a smaller road, **then continued** as the car picked up speed.

DON'T DROWN YOUR READERS IN DETAILS

~ Too much unnecessary detail complicates the issue and impedes the flow of ideas.

Leave out those picky little details that just serve to distract the reader, who wonders for an instant why they're there and if they're significant:

Before:
He **had arrived at** the vending machine and was punching the buttons **on its front with an outstretched index finger** when a voice from behind him broke **him away from** his thoughts.

After:

He was punching the buttons on the vending machine when a voice behind him broke into his thoughts.

In the first example, we have way too much minute detail. What else would he be punching the buttons with besides his finger? And we don't need to know which finger or that it's outstretched. Everybody does it pretty much the same. Avoid having minute details like this that just clutter up your prose.

Before:

The officer was indicating with a hand gesture a door that was behind and off to the right of Wilson. An angular snarl stuck to his face, he swung his head around to look in the direction the officer was pointing.

After:

The officer **gestured** to a door behind Wilson. **Snarling**, he **turned** to look behind him.

Before:

Jason motioned to a particular number in the middle of the spreadsheet that Tom currently had on the computer screen.

After:

Jason motioned to a number in the middle of the spreadsheet on the screen.

Or:

Jason pointed to a number in the middle of the spreadsheet.

Or even better:

Jason pointed to a number on the spreadsheet.

And finally:

Before:

Admiral Paul McLean strode into the room. A four-star

admiral **who currently was** commander of the US Special Operations Command **located in** Tampa, Florida, McLean directed all the Special Forces **throughout the military** from the Green Berets to the Navy SEALs.

After:
> Admiral Paul McLean strode into the room. A four-star admiral and commander of US Special Operations in Tampa, McLean directed all the Special Forces, from the Green Berets to the Navy SEALs.

CONDENSE LONG-WINDED DIALOGUE

People rarely speak in complete, grammatically correct sentences, especially when they're in a casual situation, in a hurry, upset or scared. Overly correct dialogue just doesn't sound natural. Unless you've got two professors or other professionals speaking to each other in the workplace, don't have your characters speaking in long complete sentences or in lengthy paragraphs.

In tense or rushed action scenes especially, go for incomplete sentences and one or two-word questions and answers. Read your dialogue aloud or even role-play with a friend to hear where you can cut words to make it sound more realistic.

~ Pare down dialogue to make it sound real.

Before:
> The homicide detective looked at the CSI, who was on his way out. "Leaving already?"
> "This wasn't the crime scene. Not much for me to find. **You would do me a huge favor by making sure that the next time we had a murder I had an actual crime scene to investigate.**"
> "I'll keep that in mind."

After:
> The homicide detective looked at the CSI, who was on his way out. "Leaving already?"
> "This wasn't the crime scene. Not much for me to find. **Next**

time can you get me an actual crime scene to investigate?"
"I'll keep that in mind."

Before:

"C'mon, I don't believe that. Lance knew you'd tell the cops about the connection. **He just wanted the excuse in place because he knew Perkins might not be leaving.**"

After:

"C'mon, I don't believe that. Lance knew you'd tell the cops about the connection. **He just wanted an excuse in case Perkins didn't leave.**"

Before:

Thomas flipped a page in his notebook. "Do you keep records **in your system that specify which of your inmates had access to this room?**"

After:

Thomas flipped a page in his notebook. "Do you keep records **of inmates who've had access to this room?**"

For more on making dialogue sound real, see Chapters 23 & 24.

Resources:
Jodie's editing and:
Robert W. Harris, *When Good People Write Bad Sentences*
Jessica Page Morrell, *Thanks, But This Isn't For Us*
Sol Stein, *Stein on Writing*

Chapter 17 – DANGLING PARTICIPLES, MISPLACED MODIFIERS, AND OTHER AWKWARD CONSTRUCTIONS

PROBLEMS WITH PARTICIPLES, DANGLING OR OTHERWISE

Participles are verbs that end in –ing (present participle) or –ed (past participle). According to Chicago Manual of Style, "The present participle (-ing verb) denotes the verb's action as *in progress or incomplete* at the time expressed by the sentence's principal verb." In other words, **an –ing verb expresses an action that is still taking place when another action occurs.**

For example, "As he was driving on the freeway, a police car whizzed past, lights flashing and sirens blaring." Or "She escaped while the house was still burning."

So you can't really use an –ing verb unless that action can still be taking place when the next action occurs. Here are some examples of incorrect use of participles:

LOGISTICAL IMPOSSIBILITIES

What's wrong with these sentences?

Hurrying up the sidewalk, she ran into her office building.

Dashing across the lobby, she jabbed the button for the elevator.

Tapping her toes impatiently, she dashed into a free elevator that stopped.

What's the problem ? Logistics. The -ing verb means that action is still happening, but she can't run into her office building while hurrying up the sidewalk – it's physically impossible. And if she's still dashing across the lobby, she can't be jabbing the elevator button.

Check those sentences starting with -ing verbs.

Newbie writers often start sentence after sentence with -ing verbs (participles). That's another sign of amateurish writing, and causes logistic problems. Besides being repetitive and boring, this sentence construction usually ends up describing a physically impossible series of actions – sequential actions described as if they're simultaneous, as in the examples above.

Here's another one that doesn't work:

Pulling the car over to the curb, she ran up the sidewalk.

She can't run up the sidewalk while she's pulling over to the curb. It should be something like:

She pulled the car over to the curb, parked, then ran up the sidewalk.

Or:
After pulling the car over to the curb, she jumped out and ran up the sidewalk.

So vary your sentence structure, and if you start a sentence or clause with an –ing verb, make sure it works.

WATCH FOR THOSE DANGLING PARTICIPLES

According to Merriam-Webster's Collegiate Dictionary, a participle is a word having the characteristics of both verb and adjective. As mentioned above, participles are verb forms that end in –ing or –ed, like "buzzing" or "roaring", or "satisfied" or "soaked." A participial phrase modifies a noun, like "Climbing the mountain, the hikers soon grew tired." The phrase is talking about the activity of the person or thing closest to it, in this case, the hikers, so it's correct.

Here's an example of a dangling participle: "Exploring the trails, the birds chirped merrily." It's not the birds that are exploring the trails, so it needs to be changed to something like "Exploring the trails, the hikers heard birds chirping around them."

A few more examples of dangling participles:

Wrong:

Dodging the traffic, his cell phone got dropped on the street.

It's not the cell phone that's dodging the traffic, so it needs to be:

Right:

Dodging the traffic, he dropped his cell phone on the street.

Wrong:

Gazing out the window, the willow tree swayed in the breeze.

This sentence implies it's the willow tree that is gazing out the window. It would need to be changed to something like:

Right:

Gazing out the window, she saw the willow tree swaying in the breeze.

Wrong:

Slathered in chocolate icing with sprinkles, the customers bought boxes of the sweet, decadent donuts.

It's not the customers who are slathered in icing with sprinkles! This should be changed to something like:

The customers bought boxes of the sweet, decadent donuts slathered in chocolate icing with sprinkles.

And you wouldn't want to write, "Soaked to the skin, she dried off the kids when they came in from the rain." – Unless the mom is soaked to the skin, too!

MISPLACED MODIFIERS ARE A MISTAKE

Similarly, watch where you put your descriptive phrases in sentences, as they modify the words closest to them. For example,

Wrong:

Tall and rugged, the teenage girl gazed at the basketball star in admiration.

As it is phrased here, the "tall and rugged" refers to the teenage girl, when it's supposed to be describing the basketball star. It should be rephrased to something like,

Right:

The teenage girl gazed at the tall, rugged basketball star in admiration.

PART III

FLOW AND PACING

Chapter 18 – CREATE SENTENCES THAT FLOW

Besides streamlining your writing by cutting down on wordiness and repetitions, another essential step in revising your writing style for maximum power and flow is to consider the length, variety, and structure of your sentences.

In general, it's best to vary your sentence types and lengths, not only to avoid monotony and amateurish writing, but also to enhance the impact, mood and effect you're striving for in any given scene.

My upcoming book, *The Final Polish – Putting the Finishing Touches on Your Novel*, will discuss effective, powerful sentence structure in considerably more detail. For now, here are a few quick tips for adding oomph to your sentences and paragraphs.

SOME TIPS FOR WRITING SENTENCES THAT FLOW:

~ Vary the length and structure of your sentences.

Within a paragraph, it's usually best to combine short, long, and medium-length sentences of different forms.

In general, avoid too many short, choppy sentences. Several short subject-verb-object sentences in a row can often seem amateurish, like grade-school writing.

Avoid long, convoluted sentences that force the reader to go back and reread the whole thing to get the meaning, like: "Inasmuch as I'd hoped for a reconciliation, circumstances dictated that other factors and various family members played a decisive role in the ongoing…" blah, blah.

Create Sentences That Flow

For tense scenes, it's usually more effective to use short, terse sentences, rather than long, meandering ones. And one- or two-word sentences, used judiciously, are excellent for emphasizing a point.

(Some of the "before" examples below are exaggerated to get the point across quickly.)

~ **Vary the beginnings of your sentences.**

Don't start several sentences in a row with "He" or "She," or even alternating with a name, or "The man" or "The woman," etc.:

Before:
> She was wearing a short leather skirt and a tight tank top. She had long shapely legs that seemed to go on forever. She turned to him and brushed a few strands of blond hair away from her eyes. She flashed a smile, but didn't walk toward him. She went the other way.

After:
> She was wearing a short leather skirt and a tight tank top. Her long shapely legs seemed to go on forever. She turned to him and flashed a smile, brushing a few strands of blond hair away from her eyes. But instead of walking toward him, she went the other way.

Don't start sentence after sentence with a gerund:

> Creeping to the office door, Eileen stood listening. Hearing nothing, she opened it and peeked out. Seeing no one in the hallway, she headed for the door near the entrance to the showroom. Entering the room, she turned on the light and closed the door behind her. Expecting to see a room filled with stolen artwork, Eileen was disappointed.

And for fiction, feel free to ignore that old rule about not starting a sentence with "And," "But," or "So."

~ **Rearrange the ideas for a more sophisticated feel:**

Before:

His headlights found the driveway leading to the rear of the duplex. He parked in the darkness. He closed the car door carefully after him. He drew his gun. He was relieved to see no lights in the windows. He walked quietly up the path to the back door.

After:

His headlights found the driveway leading to the rear of the duplex. He drove around, then parked in the darkness. Closing the car door carefully after him, he drew his gun and crept forward. As he walked quietly up the path to the back deck, he was relieved to see no lights in the windows.

Change up "and" sentences, which can seem clunky and amateurish.

Before:
He was tall and thin with a long narrow face and looked exhausted.

After:
Tall and thin with a long narrow face, he looked exhausted.

Before:
The bag lady wore a ragged overcoat and she trudged along, pushing a shopping cart full of junk.

After:
The bag lady, who wore a ragged overcoat, trudged along, pushing a shopping cart full of junk.

Or:
Her ragged overcoat hanging on her thin frame, the bag lady trudged along, pushing a shopping cart overloaded with junk.

Combine sentences and reword for better flow:

Before:
Ben Cross was a top-notch investigator. He was at a table drinking coffee and eating a donut when Shelley walked in.

After:

Ben Cross, a top-notch investigator, was at a table drinking coffee and eating a donut when Shelly walked in.

Or:

Shelly walked in the café and looked around. Ben Cross, a successful, well-connected security contractor, was at a table drinking coffee and eating a donut.

No run-ons:

Watch out for run-on sentences or comma splices, like "Her son was an athlete he played all sports." Or "He doesn't play football anymore, he injured his back." Fix these by inserting a period, dash, or semicolon, or a conjunction like *and, or, nor, but, for, so, as, yet, since, because*, etc., for example: "Her son was an athlete—he played all sports." Or: "He doesn't play football anymore because he injured his back."

SENTENCE STRUCTURE FOR CLARITY AND IMPACT:

~ The order the words in sentences affects the meaning.

Syntax (the order of words in a sentence) can often make the difference between confusion and clarity.

Confusing:

The last time he was anywhere near this apprehensive was years before he joined the FBI in a doctor's office with his mother.

Huh? He joined the FBI in a doctor's office?

Clear:

The last time he was anywhere near this apprehensive was in a doctor's office with his mother, years before he joined the FBI.

~ Who does that "he" or "she" refer to? Effective and clear use of pronouns.

Whenever the reader has to pause—even for a fraction of a second—to figure out who that pronoun is talking about, it takes them out of the story. Be sure to make it clear who the "he" or "she" is referring to.

Confusing:

Margaret was in the kitchen with Sherry when she told her the shocking news.

Who told whom the shocking news? The general rule is that the pronoun (he, she, etc.) refers to the last person of that gender mentioned. But will all your readers know that? It's usually best to make it clear.

Clear:

As Margaret was making coffee for them, Sherry told her the shocking news.

Confusing:

Roberto yanked José around and he kicked him.

We don't really know who did the kicking and who got kicked.

Clear:

Roberto yanked Jose around, then kicked him.

~ Show cause-effect relationships by combining into one sentence, connected by "so" or "but" or "when" or "if" or "then" or some other causal connector:

Before:

"Somebody placed a piece of cardboard over the surveillance camera. There's nothing to see until they come back to remove it."

After:

"Somebody put a piece of cardboard over the surveillance camera, so there's nothing to see until they come back to remove it."

~ To add emphasis, isolate the significant word, phrase or sentence:

For a critical idea you want readers to ponder, move the pivotal sentence down to a new line, with a space below it. This pause for significance alerts the reader to the full impact of the sentence.

Before:

Sheryl was worried. If the coroner ruled the death suspicious, that would lead to a full-scale investigation. Detective O'Reilly would turn over every stone searching for answers. What he might find could put an end to all of Sheryl's dreams.

The CSIs busied themselves around the body. Sheryl wished she were somewhere else.

After – Note how the last sentence below gains significance because it ends the paragraph and the chapter:

Sheryl had difficulty breathing.

If the coroner ruled the death suspicious, that would lead to a full-scale investigation. Detective O'Reilly would turn over every stone searching for answers.

And what he found could put an end to all her dreams.

How the Experts do it:

Here's a chapter ending by Harlan Coben in his bestselling thriller, *Play Dead*:

But of course, he could not tell Laura any of those things. She would never just accept his word. She would demand to know how he knew so much about David's drowning.

And that was something he could never tell her.

Partial sentences can also be excellent for emphasis, especially at the end of a scene or chapter, as in this chapter ending from Robert Crais' *The Sentry*:

...he told himself the violence in his life had cost him everything, but he knew that was not true. As lonely as he sometimes felt, he still had more to lose.

He could lose his best friend.

Or himself.

Chapter 19 – PICK UP THE PACE FOR A
REAL PAGE-TURNER

Don't let the story drag

Readers of fiction often complain that a book didn't keep their interest because "it dragged," or "the story meandered," or "it was slow going," or "it was boring in parts." Today's readers have shorter attention spans. Most of them/us don't have the patience for the lengthy descriptive passages, the long, convoluted "literary" sentences, or the leisurely, painstaking pacing characterized by fiction of a century or two ago.

Besides, with movies, television, the internet, and increased travel, we don't need most of the detailed descriptions of locations anymore, unlike early readers who'd perhaps never left their village or city, and had very few visual images of other locales to draw on.

We've probably all read (or at least started) novels that just seem to drag in parts, where the author has spent too much time on static description, lengthy backstory, analysis and rumination, or other explanatory lead-ups, instead of grabbing our attention and hooking us in with compelling characters faced with critical challenges, and lots of action and dialogue.

Most readers these days have little patience for an overly leisurely, analytical style, and it definitely doesn't work for suspense-thrillers, action-adventure, and most other best-selling fiction.

But nonstop frenzied action is overkill

On the other hand, I've seen movies and read a few books where it's nonstop high-speed action, filled with chases and explosions without a break. Too much of that gets old fast, making us feel overwhelmed or just numb.

So even if you're writing a fast-paced thriller or action-adventure, you don't want to write your whole book at a break-neck pace, as that can be exhausting for the reader. Give them a chance to catch their breath from time to time before the next onslaught.

Control the pace

Readers' tolerance or desire for either a leisurely pace or lots of action depends on the genre, of course. A literary fiction will usually have more thoughtful analysis and slower pacing than an action-thriller, for example. But in any successful novel, the key is to vary the pacing. And of course in "page-turning" suspense fiction, the pace should be generally brisk, with lots of conflict and tension.

William Noble, in *Conflict, Action & Suspense,* says, "Story pace essentially means two things: smooth, event writing without anticlimaxes, without lengthy static prose; and carefully constructed scenes that blend with one another and build to a satisfying climax."

So it's important to learn techniques to control the pace in your story, where to speed it up and where to slow it down, weighing each individual scene against the whole story line.

Skip the boring bits

While you don't want your story barreling along at a break-neck speed all the way through, you do want the pace to be generally brisk enough to keep the readers' interest. As Elmore Leonard said, "I try to leave out the parts that people skip."

Cut to the chase

To increase the pace and overall tension of your story, it's a good idea to cut back on setup and backstory. Here's what Donald Maass has to say about setup: "'Setup' is, by definition, not story. It always drags. Always. Leave it out. Find another way." Some backstory can be essential, but marble it in in bits and pieces, on an "as-needed" basis, rather than interrupting the story for paragraphs or pages of explanation of character background.

So to increase the pace, keep your descriptive passages short and vivid, and concentrate on scenes with action, dialogue, and lots of tension. Also, show, don't tell – use vivid, sensory imagery. Use a direct, lean writing style, and just leave out the boring bits.

CONCRETE TIPS FOR PICKING UP THE PACE

Here are a few easy techniques for accelerating your narrative style at strategic spots to create those tense, fast-paced scenes. We'll start from the macro level of chapters and scenes, then zooming in to the micro level of paragraphs, sentences, and words.

A.   CREATING SCENES AND CHAPTERS

~ Take out, rewrite, or condense chapters and scenes that drag.

Do you have any chapters or scenes where not much is happening? Any slow-moving scenes without enough tension or change should be condensed, rewritten, or even deleted. You can reduce any essentials from the scene to a paragraph or two, or even just a few sentences, and tack that on to the beginning or end of another scene.

~ Keep chapters and scenes short.

This will help sustain the readers' interest and keep them turning the pages. James Patterson is a master at short chapters, and his followers seem to really like that. Especially good for reluctant or busy readers.

~ Start each scene or chapter as late as possible.

Don't open with a lengthy lead-up. Your story and every scene and chapter should start with some kind of question, conflict or intrigue, to arouse the curiosity of the reader and make them want to keep reading. The Latin term *in medias res* means "to start in the middle." Doesn't have to be right in the middle, but no need to rev your motors for too long, or spend a lot of time setting up the scene. Jump right in to the action.

~ Open each scene with a question, and use intrigue, change or conflict.

I don't mean to start literally with a question ending in a question mark, but start with an intriguing statement or situation that piques the reader's curiosity and makes them want to find the answer or outcome.

~ Show critical, compelling scenes in real time.

Where you want to pick up the pace, use mainly actions and dialogue, and minimal or no reflection, analyses, explanations, and description, and reduce or skip over slower transition scenes. (Show, don't tell.)

~ Use summary to get past the boring bits, or skip ahead for effect.

Summarize in a sentence or two a passage of time where nothing much happens, to transition quickly from one critical scene to the next: "Three days later, he was no further ahead."

Skip past all the humdrum details and transition info, like getting from one place to another, and jump straight to the next action scene. Your protagonist leaves her house. Add an extra space, then show her fighting traffic or at her workplace office having an argument with her boss. No need to show her getting into her car, driving to her destination, etc. The reader can easily fill in the gaps.

~ Make sure every scene has enough conflict.

Every page should have tension. Conflict and tension are what drive fiction forward and keep readers turning the pages. See Chapter 5 of my book, *Writing a Killer Thriller – An Editor's Guide to Writing Powerful Fiction.*

~ Every scene needs a change of some kind.

No scene should be static. Throw a wrench in the works, make something unexpected happen. Show your character being challenged and forced to change in some way. Add new characters, new information, new dangers.

Change pushes a story forward. See Chapter 4 of my book *Writing a Killer Thriller*.

~ Don't drag out chapter endings.

End each scene or chapter as early as possible, rather than spending a lot of time wrapping up. And don't tie up the events in a nice, neat little bow – that will just encourage the reader to close the book rather than to keep reading in anticipation. Instead, end in uncertainty or a new problem.

~ Use cliff-hangers.

For fast pacing and more tension and intrigue, end most scenes and chapters with unresolved issues, with some kind of twist, revelation, story question, intrigue, challenge, setback or threat. Prolonging the outcome, putting the resolution off to another chapter piques the readers' curiosity and makes them worry, which keeps them turning the pages.

~ Employ scene cuts or jump cuts.

Create a series of short, unresolved incidents that occur in rapid succession. Stop at a tantalizing moment and jump to a different scene, often at a different time and place, with different characters – perhaps picking up from a scene you cut short earlier. Jump-cutting is a more extreme version of skipping ahead. This is used a lot in movies. You jump straight from one scene to another, with no transitioning at all in between.

Switch chapters or scenes quickly back and forth between your protagonist and antagonist(s), or from one dicey, uncertain situation to another. Don't resolve the conflict/problem before you switch to the next one.

Robert Dugoni uses this technique masterfully in his legal thriller, *Murder One*, where he abruptly stops chapters and scenes at critical moments and leaves us hanging while he jumps to a new nail-biting scene, with no transition.

B. PACING WITHIN SCENES

~ Limit explaining – Show, don't tell.

Keep descriptive passages, expository passages, lengthy backstory, and ruminations, reflections and analyses to a minimum. Action scenes need to be "shown" in real time, to make them more immediate and compelling, rather than "telling" about them after the fact. Use lots of action and dialogue. Don't have the character *telling* the reader about an event or how she's feeling about it. *Show* her actions and feelings directly.

~ Use shorter paragraphs and more white space.

Short paragraphs and frequent paragraphing create more white space. The eye moves down the page faster, so the mind does, too. This also increases the tension, which is always a good thing in fiction.

~ Use rapid-fire dialogue, with conflict, confrontations, power struggles, suspicion.

Use short questions, abrupt, oblique or evasive answers, incomplete sentences, one or two-word responses, and little or no description, deliberation or reflection. As Sol Stein points out, "In fiction, a quick exchange of adversarial dialogue often proves to be an ideal way of picking up the pace."

Here's an example from *The Watchman* by best-selling author Robert Crais. One of my favorite heroes, Joe Pike, is protecting a wealthy young girl from enemies who are closing in. Pike starts out.

"Pack your things. We're going to see Bud."

She lowered the coffeepot, staring at him as if she were fully dressed.

"I thought we were safe here."

"We are. But if something happens, we'll want our things."

"What's going to happen?"

"Every time we leave the house, we'll take our things. That's the way it is."

"I don't want to ride around all day scrunched in your car.

98

Can't I stay here?"

"Get dressed. We have to hurry."

"But you told him noon. Universal is only twenty minutes away."

"Let's go. We have to hurry."

She stomped back into the kitchen and threw the pot into the sink.

"Your coffee sucks!"

"We'll get Starbucks."

She didn't seem so wild, even when she threw things.

We get the undercurrent of tension in Joe, who's trying to hustle her out without alarming her.

C.   WRITE TIGHT WITHIN PARAGRAPHS

Next, analyze the pacing at a micro level and tighten up your paragraphs and sentences, eliminating repetitions and reducing convoluted phrasing and excess wordiness.

~ Use powerful sentences with concrete, sensory words that evoke emotional responses.

Utilize the strongest, most concrete word you can find for the situation. Avoid vague, wishy-washy or abstract words, and unfamiliar terms the reader may have to look up. Concentrate on evocative, to-the-point verbs and nouns, and cut way back on adjectives, adverbs and prepositions. Also, take out all unnecessary, repetitive words and those wishy-washy, humdrum "filler" words and phrases. And use plenty of sensory details, emotional and physical reactions, and *attitude*. Here are a few examples of sentences that meander too much to capture the tension of the moment.

Setup: A tense, edgy scene in a bar. As originally written, it's too wordy and conversational, when terse would be more effective to mirror the anxiety and stress of the situation:

Before:

Then he continued, speaking just loudly enough to be heard by Thomas but not by any of the surrounding drinkers, not that anyone seemed to be listening. "Here's what we're going to do," he said.

After:

Then he continued in a low voice, "Here's what we're going to do."

Or, disguised from another book I edited:

Before:

Christine fired him a dirty look, probably because he was doing this in piecemeal and not getting straight to the point as she would have liked him to. Her voice was terse. "Why not?"

After:

Christine fired him a dirty look as if to say, *Cut to the chase.* Her voice was terse. "Why not?"

Or just:

Christine fired him a dirty look. "Why not?"

~ Vary sentence structure, and shorten sentences for effect.

Shorter sentences give a pause so the reader focuses more on the impact of the previous sentence or the steps involved or whatever. Don't run a bunch of significant ideas together in one long sentence, as they each will be diminished a bit, lost in among all the other ideas presented. You can also go to a new line and add paragraphing for the same effect.

For a fast-paced, scary scene, use short, clipped sentences, as opposed to long, meandering, leisurely ones. Sentence fragments are very effective for increasing the tension and pace. Like this. It really works. Especially in dialogue.

Here's a compelling, chilling passage from Alex Kava's *The Soul Catcher*, about a young woman being strangled:

No air. She couldn't breathe. Her feet kicked, then slipped

out from under her.

She couldn't regain her balance. Couldn't see. Couldn't breathe. Her knees wouldn't work. Her arms flayed. Her fingers dug even deeper into her own skin, but nothing helped. When blackness came, it came as a relief.

And a brief passage from *White Hot,* a thriller by one of my favorite authors, Sandra Brown. The tension is obvious.

At the door of the motel room, she pushed the key into the lock.

"You're out late."

Nearly jumping out of her skin, she spun around to find Chris standing close. It was as though he had materialized out of thin air.

"What do you want, Chris?"

"Can I come in?"

"What for?"

"I want to talk to my sister."

His disarming smile left her cold. "About what?"

"Invite me in and I'll tell you. He held up a bottle. "I brought wine."

~ Make your point, then move on.

Don't belabor the point or say it several ways.

~ Use active voice instead of passive to add urgency:

"The detectives questioned the suspects," rather than "The suspects were questioned by the detectives." Or "The tornado leveled the resort," rather than "The resort was leveled by the tornado."

Resources:
Donald Maass, *Writing the Breakout Novel*
Sol Stein, *Stein on Writing*
Jodie's fiction reading and editing

Chapter 20 – PACING FOR POWER – EXPAND THE MOMENT TO INCREASE TENSION & SUSPENSE

Using style and pacing techniques to expand critical moments to increase tension and suspense:

In Chapter 19, we discussed techniques for picking up the pace in your novel to create a real "page turner." But sometimes, at a critical, tense or emotional moment of a story, you actually want to expand time, to slow things down to give the reader a chance to realize the significance of the problem and appreciate the challenges the character is facing to overcome the obstacles.

This stretching-out technique also increases the tension, draws out the suspense and intrigue, and emotionally engages the readers to get their adrenaline flowing. So don't zip past those crucial pivoting moments of the story. Milk them for all they're worth.

~ Show every little critical detail at times of life or death.

This is an especially good technique if you have your protagonist trapped and trying to escape before being caught or killed. She's looking around her, trying to find something – anything – that can help her escape the situation on time. Show every little detail as she desperately scans her surroundings, the clock ticking away before she's found by the killer.

Or perhaps he or she is trying to solve a puzzle or discover someone's true identity, but time is running out. Stretch out the search, showing each detail.

~ Build up anticipation before an important discovery by adding more detail to slow time down and show every step taken before an important discovery:

In the "before" example, there's not enough lead-up or details to effectively build reader interest before the important discovery. Best to build up to the final discovery to add tension, suspense and intrigue.

Before:
>   Val searched the bureau and the nightstand, then dropped to all fours to dig beneath the bed. Glad she did, because that's where she found Mrs. MacPherson's old love letters from Charles Rutledge, hidden in a wooden box, dated around the time of their graduation. Unfortunately, they made no mention of a pregnancy.

After:
>   Val searched the bureau drawers, looking for some connection—a diary or old love letters. She rifled through some underwear and discovered an envelope. She peered inside. Photos. She rifled through them quickly—just pictures of Mrs. MacPherson's grandchildren. *Damn.* Time was running out—they'd be back soon and she couldn't be caught here.

>   She quickly crossed to the window and peered out the edge of it. Still clear. She approached the bed and rifled through the nightstand. Nothing but a flashlight, aspirin and sleep meds. She glanced at the bedside clock, then looked around, desperate. There had to be some kind of proof of their involvement somewhere. Where could it be?

>   She dropped to all fours and peered underneath the bed. Amongst the dust and cobwebs she saw some old shoes. As she pushed them aside, her hand hit a wooden box. She grasped it and pulled it out. It had an old metal latch. She tried it and it opened.

>   Inside was a bunch of old letters tied with a ribbon. And a thick envelope. She opened the envelope to find old high school photos, many in black and white. She grabbed the pack of letters, slipped one out from the ribbon, and opened it. Bingo! It was from Carson Granger, and dated around the time of their graduation. Unfortunately, they made no mention of a pregnancy.

~ Isolate a sentence, phrase, or word to underline its importance.

Separating one long sentence into two to emphasize the beginning or the ending is a great technique. Or start a new paragraph. Or even drop down and put that word, phrase or sentence on its own line, with an extra space or two after it, to make the reader pause and fully realize the significance of that last sentence. Even better, end the scene or chapter there.

A disguised example from my editing:

Before:
> The pickup sped away in a cloud of dust, leaving him alone in the middle of the desert, sweltering under the hot sun, with no food or water.

After:
> The pickup sped away in a cloud of dust, leaving him alone in the desert. He stood up and looked in every direction. No sign of another human being, as far as the eye could see.
>
> And he was already sweltering under the hot sun. No shade in sight.
>
> They'd left him nothing to eat.
>
> And worse—not a drop of water.

Following are various techniques to maximize the tension, suspense and intrigue to take a scene from ho-hum to riveting.

TIPS FOR INCREASING TENSION AND SUSPENSE BY SLOWING DOWN PACING

~ **Write longer, more involved sentences.** This forces the reader to pay more attention and concentrate on every word.

~ **Use compelling imagery and to-the-point description** to show exactly how and why the setting, circumstances, and characters are significant and ominous.

~ **Exploit setting details to maximum effect** by using darkness, shadows, harsh weather, eerie stillness, ominous sounds, suspicious smells, etc.

~ **Make time pass in slow motion** to create anticipation, anxiety, and rising tension.

~ **Move the camera lens in close and show critical details** that seem "off" or could help the character in some way.

~ **Heighten the senses of the POV character** and show the results – tell us every little sight, sound and smell they're picking up, since what they perceive could be critical to their survival.

~ **Don't skip over anything important.** To increase tension and worry, draw out the moment and show every step of their struggle to solve the problem on time or escape the situation before it's too late.

~ **Let us know what the POV character is thinking** and worrying about, analyzing and planning.

~ **Show your characters' increased apprehension and other heightened emotional reactions** to what's going on around them.

~ **Pause for significance.** Isolate critical info on its own line, so the reader doesn't miss it.

PART IV

FIND FRESH, VIBRANT WORDS

Chapter 21 – CHOOSE WORDS THAT NAIL IT

To bring your characters and scenes to life in a way readers can relate to, it's critical to choose just the right nuance of meaning to fit the character, action and situation. Say you've got a character walking. How are they moving? There's a huge difference between *strolling* and *striding* and *shuffling* and *sauntering* and *slinking* and *strutting* and *sashaying* and *slogging along*, for example.

For help in zeroing in on the very best word to convey the tone and mood you're after, it's a good idea to use both a thesaurus and a dictionary (either online or print). Use the thesaurus to find a wide range of possibilities, then if you're not 100% sure of the meaning, check with the dictionary to avoid embarrassing slip-ups.

WORDS: REPLACE BLAH WITH ZING

~ The Thesaurus is Your Friend – Really!

Do you ever draw a blank when you're trying to find just the right word to fit a situation in your fiction or nonfiction writing? It's on the tip of your tongue but you just can't think of it. That's where the trusty thesaurus comes in. Look up the most ordinary or closest word to the one you need, and you'll find similar words you can then use to narrow down to "le mot juste" – the one that perfectly expresses what you're looking for.

~ But don't choose words your readers will need to look up in a dictionary.

The thesaurus sometimes gets a bad rap because of writers who get carried away trying to find a more original way to express something and end up replacing good, solid, concrete words with little-known abstract or esoteric words that evoke no emotion and often annoy or confuse the reader. For example, avoid using pretentious words like *abscise* instead of cut or snip, or *mendacious* instead of dishonest or lying.

But if used judiciously, the thesaurus can be an indispensable guide for helping you enrich your language and imagery and write more powerfully – and keep the readers absorbed in your story. And by avoiding trite, everyday, overused words that have lost their power, you keep your imagery fresh and your story compelling.

Just make sure to choose a word that really nails the wording you're looking for, not one that will impress your readers with your literary prowess. Choosing obscure words that just draw attention to themselves is a sure way to distract readers from your story and annoy them. So read your story out loud later to make sure the words you've chosen sound natural and are words you and your characters would actually use in everyday situations.

Example:

"Perhaps Jake's **hubris** is a good thing. It's the one thing we have going for us."

Jodie's comment in the margin: Many readers won't know what *hubris* means, and it's not commonly used in casual conversation. I'd say "arrogance" or "pride" or "overconfidence" or "confidence."

CHOOSE WORDS THAT ENHANCE THE TONE, MOOD, AND VOICE OF YOUR SCENE

FIND VIVID VERBS

Verbs are especially important, as there are so many variations in the way someone can move or speak or eat or whatever, depending on their personality, mood, age, gender, size, background, health, fitness level, and of course the circumstances. So it's worth the effort to find just the right verb that nails the action and makes sense in the context of the scene. A verb that doesn't quite fit can be jarring and turn a reader off, whereas finding a stronger, more specific verb can really strengthen a scene, resulting in greater reader involvement and enjoyment.

PEOPLE IN MOTION

For example, check out how many ways you can say "walked" or "moved." (Hint – look up the present tense – "walk" or "move.") You can use an online thesaurus or go all out and buy the best print one out there – J.I. Rodale's *The Synonym Finder*, which, at a hefty 1361 pages long, is without a doubt the most comprehensive thesaurus in book form in the English language. (Thanks to Jessica Page Morrell for turning me on to this indispensable aid for writers.)

For the verb "walked" for example, Rodale gives us a long list of great synonyms to help us capture just the right situation and tone. He just lists them, but here I've roughly categorized some of them to suit various situations, and changed them to past tense, to suit most novels and short stories.

~ WORDS FOR "WALKED"

Situations:

Drunk, drugged, wounded, ill: lurched, staggered, wobbled, shuffled, shambled

Urgent, purposeful, concerned, stressed: strode, paced, treaded, moved, went, advanced, proceeded, marched, stepped

Relaxed, wandering: strolled, sauntered, ambled, wandered, roamed, roved, meandered, rambled, traipsed

Tired: trudged, plodded, slogged, clopped, shuffled, tramped

Rough terrain, hiking: marched, trooped, tramped, hiked

Sneaking, stealth: sidled, slinked, minced, tiptoed, tread softly

Showing off: strutted, paraded, sashayed
Other walking situations: waddled, galumphed (moved with a clumsy, heavy tread), shambled, wended, tiptoed

So in general, it's best to avoid plain vanilla verbs like "walked" or "went" if you can find a more specific word to evoke just the kind of movement you're trying to describe.

~ But don't grab that synonym too quickly! Watch out for show-offy or silly words.

After you've found a list of interesting synonyms, choose carefully which one to use for the situation, as well as the overall tone of your book. For example, for "walk," don't go to extremes by choosing little-known, pretentious words like "ambulate" and "perambulate" and "peregrinate" (!), or overly colloquial, slang, or regional expressions like "go by shank's mare" and "hoof it."

~ And beware of words that just don't fit that situation.

Also, some synonyms are too specific for general use, so they can be jarring if used in the wrong situations. I had two author clients who seemed to like to use "shuffled" for ordinary, healthy people walking around. To me, "shuffled" conjures up images of a patient moving down the hallway of a hospital, pushing their IV, or an old person moving around their kitchen in their slippers. Don't have your cop or PI or CEO shuffling! Unless they're sick or exhausted – or half-asleep.

Similarly, I had a client years ago who was writing about wartime, and where he meant to have soldiers and officers "striding" across a room or grounds or battlefield, he had them "strutting." To me, you wouldn't say "he strutted" unless it was someone full of himself or showing off. It's definitely not an alternate word for "walked with purpose" as is "he strode."

Also, be careful of having someone "march" into a room, unless they're in the military or really fuming or determined. "Strode" captures that idea of a purposeful or determined walk better.

Or, disguised from another novel I edited:

Joe stood up, shocked and numb, after his boss delivered the tragic news about the death of his friend. He dreaded his visit to Paul's widow. He *sauntered* back to his office, his mind spinning.

Jodie's comment: "sauntered" is way too relaxed and casual a word for the situation. The guy's just been told his friend is dead. Maybe "found his way" or "stumbled" back to his office.

So after you've found a few possible words in the thesaurus, it wouldn't be a bad idea to check the exact meaning in your dictionary. For that, I recommend Merriam-Webster's Collegiate Dictionary (mine has 1622 pages). Or of course use any reputable online dictionary.

~ REPLACEMENTS FOR "RUN"

I found a list of synonyms for run, just listed in alphabetical order, then reordered them here to fit specific circumstances:

Situations:

Fun, play: amble, skip, scamper, scoot

Start off running: take off, bolt, make a break, light out, make off, dash, tear out, make tracks, split

Tense, frightened, being chased: barrel, dart, escape, flee, dash, hurry, race, rush, escape, flee, hasten, hustle, speed, sprint, scramble, scurry, tear

Athletic training, exercise: jog, pace, race, dash, sprint, travel

In a hurry: hasten, bustle, hurry, hustle, rush, dash, hasten, scurry

Animals: scamper, trot, scurry, take flight, travel

Colloquial, humorous: hotfoot it, skedaddle, make tracks, scoot, take off, tear out

And serendipitously, I was just reading Robert Crais's thriller, *The Last Detective,* and discovered another great list of synonyms for "run." The anonymous narrator is describing a recurring dream:

"I am desperate to escape this place. I want to beat feet, boogie, truck, book, haul ass, motor, shred, jet, jam, split, cut out, blow, roll, abandon, get away, get gone, scram, RUN…"

But proceed with caution. Again, once you have the list, choose your word carefully. Obviously, if you've got someone running for their life, you wouldn't use such light-hearted synonyms as "scamper" or "scoot" or "skip" or "trot" or "amble."

And it's also important to consider the overall voice of the scene and the inner thoughts of the viewpoint character. Are they the kind of person who would use "skedaddle" or "hotfoot it" in their personal vocabulary?

~ DIFFERENT WAYS OF LOOKING

Try looking up the verb "look" in a good thesaurus. Here are some of the synonyms J.I. Rodale lists:

see, visualize, behold, notice, take in, regard, observe, study, inspect, examine, contemplate, eye, check out, scrutinize, review, monitor, scan, view, survey, scout, sweep, watch, observe, witness, gaze, peer, glance, glimpse, ogle, leer, stare, goggle, gape, gawk, squint, take a gander, spy, peek, peep, steal a glance at, glare, glower, look down at, look daggers… (and the list goes on).

Again, choose carefully.

Some of these, and others he lists, are just too specific or archaic for general use in fiction, so proceed with caution. For example, don't use "behold" for "look" in your present-day thriller or mystery! And "reconnoiter" works for military situations, but not for everyday use. Also, watch for eyes doing weird physical things, like "his eyes bounced around the room."

Also, there are a lot of nuances for showing a character looking at someone or something. The verbs "glare," "glance," "scan," "peer," "study," and "gaze" have quite different meanings, for example.

Before:

Brock **glared** at the intruder with the gun, **eyes wide with fear**. He shifted his stare to Gord, mouthing, "Help."

"Glared" doesn't go with "eyes wide with fear." Glared is for anger. Maybe "stared" here? And "shifted his gaze"? Or maybe:

Brock's eyes widened with fear at the intruder with the gun. He shifted his gaze to Gord, mouthing, "Help."

Similarly,

At the funeral, the widow caught Peter's glance and **squinted her eyes in accusation**. She no doubt held him responsible for her husband's death.

"Squinted" is like against the bright sun. I'd say "narrowed her eyes" or "glared at him."

NAIL IT WITH JUST THE RIGHT WORD

Here are some examples of verbs that didn't quite fit the situation. I've taken the basic idea from my fiction editing but changed the names and altered the circumstances to protect the confidentiality of my clients. The comments after each example are from my notes in the margin of the manuscript. (My italics, so you can find the word quickly.)

A high-ranking Nazi officer is about to invade the home of a wealthy Jewish family during the Second World War. The author wrote:

He *giggled* inwardly, thinking about the chaos he was about to bring to the Jews who lived here.

My comment to the writer was: The verb "giggled" fits a couple of schoolgirls, not a nasty Nazi. I suggest "smirked" or "gloated."

And don't use casual, relaxed language in a stressful situation. Choose words that reflect the urgency, tension and conflict.

Before:
David's cell phone rang. It was his wife Carole, who was

three blocks away in her office, babbling hysterically. He yelled for his colleague Todd, grabbed his jacket and headed for the elevator. When they got to street level, David took off *jogging* towards Carole's office building. Todd *ran comfortably* by his side. When they got there, he found the area crawling with police.

Jodie's comment: Best to not use words like "comfortably" or "jogging" at a time of stress. Choose words that fit the anxious mood and tone of the moment better.

One possibility:

...When they got to street level, David took off running towards Carole's office building. Todd raced to catch up.

BUT JUST SAY "HE SAID" AND "SHE SAID"

Don't start using a bunch of fancy synonyms for "said." Best to just use "he (or she) said" most of the time, as words like "postulated" and "uttered" and "articulated" can be laughable and distracting, whereas "said" gets the meaning across without drawing attention to itself.

Start your own thesaurus and become a wordsmith.

Why not open your own Word file and call it "Thesaurus" or "Synonyms," then start lists for the verbs you use most in your writing, like *walk, move, look, run*, etc. That way you can quickly find lots of variations and try them on for size. Just don't get carried away and start using words nobody's heard of, or that don't fit the situation!

Chapter 22 – CUT THOSE CLICHÉS – MOST OF THE TIME

What's a cliché, exactly? According to the *American Heritage* online dictionary, a cliché is "a trite expression or idea."

And *Wikipedia* says, "A cliché or cliche is an expression, idea, or element that has been overused to the point of losing its original meaning or effect, especially when at some earlier time it was considered meaningful or novel. [...] Most phrases now considered clichéd were originally regarded as striking, but lost their force through overuse."

In fiction, characters and plots can be overdone to the point of becoming clichéd. Some stereotypical character types are the tall, dark, handsome hero; the gorgeous blonde; the absent-minded professor; the rumpled, quirky detective with the buxom secretary; the strong silent hero; the mean stepmother; and the gum-chewing, sassy waitress.

And basic story plots keep reappearing, too, like the Cinderella-type poor girl who finds the man of her dreams and is swept away into a new life, à la *Pygmalion* / *My Fair Lady* or Julia Roberts in *Pretty Woman*; or the stranger riding into town to save the day.

Come to think of it, Lee Child has made a very successful career on his variations of the stranger, Jack Reacher, rolling into town, unaware of a critical situation where someone is being threatened or terrorized. Reacher jumps right in and uses his considerable skills and physical prowess to find who's responsible and rid the town of the scum that are threatening them, using his unique, no-holds-barred, vigilante-style justice. Then, when peace is restored, he moves on.

Which just goes to show that using a familiar framework or premise to craft a new, exciting story can still work – over and over. Maybe there's a comfort level to a familiar plot, like eating mac and cheese. But be sure to put your own creative twist on it.

Best to cut most of those clichéd expressions.

Here, we'll just talk about those old trite descriptions and sayings, clichéd phrases like "a dark and stormy night" or "love at first sight" or "easy as pie" (which I never understood, since pie is not that easy to make!) or "scared to death" or "cute as a button" or "blind as a bat" or "dead as a doornail" or "busy as bees" or "skinny as a broom." Hackneyed expressions like these have long since lost all their zing from overuse. Now they just fall flat and can quickly mark you as an amateur writer.

So be careful not to use exhausted terms that have no oomph left in them. To give your writing zing and appeal, stay away from those boring platitudes and brainstorm for fresh word combinations with striking, vibrant imagery.

Put your own twist on them?

One trick I've seen a few authors do is start with an old cliché and change it up a bit for a new twist on an "oldie but goodie" (to use another old favorite of mine). A fresh take on a saying in a popular song of 2012 is "too school for cool," a variation on "too cool for school." (This slight-change trick can sometimes be risky, though, as readers might think you got the original saying wrong!)

I had two bananas lying on the counter the other day, touching closely, as I was using that old trick of pushing a ripe banana snug in to a green one to make the green one ripen faster. As I saw them snuggled in there, it seemed they fit the idea of "spooning" better than spoons touching. But would readers get it if I said "bananaing"? Probably not. Some of you wordsmiths might find a better way to introduce this variation on "spooning;" though.

But keep those clichés in dialogue or narration.

Clichés can work well in first-person narration or in dialogue, though, to help you create quirky, interesting characters. If you have a character telling their own story, their voice should be casual and authentic, with their individual quirks and personality shining through, so go ahead and use any clichés you think that type of person is likely to use.

Same with dialogue in third-person narration, especially if the person speaking is older, less educated, or lives in rural area. If you're depicting someone's grandpa or grandma, or an old farmer or truck driver, jump right in with those funny old expressions they're likely to use, like "Don't count your chickens before they're hatched, sonny," or "That'll kill two birds with one stone," or "Don't look a gift horse in the mouth," or "They're living high on the hog," or "He's about to kick the bucket."

And how about, "Why, when I was knee-high to a grasshopper," or "It's like looking for a needle in a haystack," or "He's like a fox in the henhouse"? These old familiar expressions are part of our cultural heritage, so sprinkle them in here and there in dialogue for effect – as long as they fit the character and situation!

In fact, bestselling author Karin Slaughter's riveting thriller, *Indelible*, starts off like this:

> "Well, look what the cat dragged in," Marla Simms bellowed, giving Sara a pointed look over her silver-rimmed bifocals. The secretary for the police station held a magazine in her arthritic hands,...

The cliché helps us get an immediate picture of the older woman.

In an excellent YA fiction I'm editing now, the nosy older neighbor lady has been asked to keep an eye on the 16-year-old protagonist who's been grounded, and the neighbor tells her she'll be watching her, "so mind your p's and q's." The cliché is perfect for characterizing the older lady and her busybody attitude.

In fact, in any kind of casual conversation between friends, as in real life, sometimes it's easiest and quickest to use a well-known expression to get your idea or point across quickly. In the middle of chatting with a friend, do we stop to think of a more original way to say something? Not usually. So neither will your characters, a lot of the time. And quirky, pet expressions are a great way to give each of your characters their own unique personality and speaking style.

A few relatively recent expressions I still enjoy hearing or reading are "She's getting her ducks in a row" and "That's on my bucket list." Sometimes a well-known expression is a perfect way to get your meaning across quickly and with a bit of attitude or local color, without going into a long explanation of what you mean.

I've just finished reading Lee Child's recent Jack Reacher thriller, *The Affair*, and in it Reacher uses the expression, "dollars to doughnuts," a few times. I don't recall if he used this expression in other books in the series, but it's kind of endearing. And another MP he's working with says, referring to how they both came to the same conclusion, "Great minds think alike. Or fools never differ." It shows a relaxed familiarity and captures what he's trying to say in a nutshell, without a long explanation. In cases like that, a just-right cliché is okay now and then. Just don't pick one of the really overused ho-hum ones that have completely lost their power, like "neat as a pin" (how can a pin be neat, anyway?) or "fit as a fiddle," which also makes no sense at all to me.

How about you? Do you have any clichés that "drive you up the wall" or "bore you to tears"? Any that you're absolutely sick of reading in fiction? Or any that you still like or use yourself for nostalgic reasons, because your mom or dad or grandparents used them, or because they've still got a bit of life left in them and they nail what you're trying to express in only a few words, without a lot of effort? Or maybe they'd be great for portraying an eccentric character. How about a cliché that you've breathed new life into by twisting it a bit?

PART V

AIM FOR AUTHENTIC DIALOGUE & THOUGHTS

Chapter 23 – REPLICATE DIALOGUE THAT'S REAL AND RIVETING

Dialogue is one of the first things agents and editors look at when they receive a manuscript for consideration. If the dialogue is wooden, stilted, and artificial, most agents will assume that the rest of the writing is amateurish, and the manuscript will be quickly rejected. Here are some concrete ways to make your dialogue more compelling and natural-sounding.

DIALOGUE NEEDS TENSION, CONFLICT, AND EMOTION!

This one is huge. As Randy Ingermanson and Peter Economy say in *Writing Fiction for Dummies*, "Dialogue is war! Every dialogue should be a controlled conflict between at least two characters with opposing agendas. The main purpose of dialogue is to advance the conflict of the story."

1. Skip the yadda-yadda.

Leave out the "Hi, how are you?" "I'm fine, and you?" "Nice day," stuff, and cut to the chase. Skip past introductions and all that empty blah-blah small talk.

2. Don't lecture.

Avoid any kind of long monologue or dialogue that just imparts information, with no tension or emotion.

3. Ban the boring bits.

Don't use dialogue as "filler" – if it doesn't advance the plot, heighten the conflict, or deepen the characterization, take it out.

4. Show the tension.

Include lots of emotional or sexual tension and subtext in your dialogue. Silence, interrupting, or abruptly changing the subject can be effective, too.

LOOSEN UP THE LANGUAGE

The most common problem with dialogue for new writers is that it often sounds too stiff and formal. Here are some easy, quick tips for loosening up the dialogue to make it sound more natural:

1. Read your dialogue out loud.

Does it sound natural? Can you cut some words out, or use more common, everyday conversational words, rather than more "correct" words? In conversation, use "bought" rather than "purchased," "use" rather than "utilize," etc.

2. Use contractions.

Change *I am* to *I'm, cannot* to *can't, we will* to *we'll, do not* to *don't, they will* to *they'll*, etc.

3. Break up those long, grammatically correct complete sentences.

Nobody talks in complete sentences in informal conversations with friends (or enemies) and family, especially in stressful situations. Frequently, use some short sentence fragments, and one-word answers.

4. Don't have one person go on and on about a subject.

Fiction is not the place for a lecture on a topic, or somebody speaking at length about himself. It's not natural, and your readers aren't interested in long monologues! Have the other person interrupt to ask a question, give their opinion, seek clarification, change the subject, disagree, etc.

KEEP IT REAL! AVOID THE OLD AYKB: "AS YOU KNOW, BOB,"

Avoid unnatural dialogue caused by having the characters say things they would never say, just to impart some information to the readers!

An extreme example of this would be a wife saying to her husband:

"As you know, we met in junior year in college and got married three years later."

Or even the more subtle, "As your lifelong friend, I must advise you…"

Using dialogue this way to get some information across to the reader is artificial and a sure sign of an amateur writer. Work the information in subtly, without having one character say something that the other would obviously already know.

EVERYBODY SPEAKS DIFFERENTLY

Give each character their own speaking style. Make sure all your characters don't sound the same (like the author).

~ Age, education, background, region, etc.

First, pay attention to differences in gender, age, social status, education, geographical location, historical era, etc. Some characters, especially professionals, will use more correct English and longer sentences, while others will use rougher language, with a lot of one- or two-word questions or answers, sprinkled with expletives.

~ Show personality differences.

Then, think about individual personality differences within that social group, and the situation.

Is your character: Shy or outgoing? Talkative or quiet? Formal or casual? Modern or old-fashioned? Confident or nervous? Tactful or blunt? Serious or lighthearted? Relaxed or stressed?

And give each character their own little quirks and slang expressions, but exercise caution when using slang or expletives. (See Chapter 19 for more on this.)

PAY ATTENTION TO GENDER DIFFERENCES

Bear in mind that men and women tend to express themselves differently.

~ Men are usually terser and more direct.

They often prefer to talk about things rather than people or feelings, and they often use brief or one-word answers.

~ Women often prefer to talk about people and relationships.

Also, they often hint at or talk around a subject, tend to express themselves in more complete sentences, and often want to discuss their feelings.

These differences are especially important to keep in mind if you're a female author writing dialogue for male characters, and vice-versa.

MORE TIPS FOR EFFECTIVE DIALOGUE

1. Avoid "talking heads" – pages of unbroken dialogue, with little action or description.

- Move the characters around the scene, and indicate their reactions, gestures and body language:

They pulled up in front of the police station. He crossed his arms. She got up and started pacing. He touched her arm. She gasped in alarm. He clenched his fists. And so on.

2. For dialogue tags, use mainly *he said* and *she said* (and *asked* for questions).

These simple indicators are non-intrusive, unlike more show-offy words like articulated, conjectured, queried, interjected, insinuated, pronounced, and uttered, which draw attention to themselves and can be annoying.

~ **Some exceptions:** In addition to *he said* and *she said*, words like *shouted, whispered, mumbled, yelled, murmured,* and *screamed* are very useful for advancing the plot and ramping up your imagery.

3. You can't smile or frown words.

Beware of using non-speaking words as attributes, as in these incorrect examples:

Not:

> "That's so nice," she smiled.

> "You bet," he grinned.

Characters can't "smile" or "grin" words!

But you can say,

> "That's so nice," she said, smiling.

> "You bet." He grinned and waved as he pulled away.

5. Avoid the dialogue tag if it's obvious who's speaking.

"Who was that on the phone?"

"Krystal."

6. But do make it clear who's speaking.

Don't go on too long without indicating the speaker. Readers don't want to have to interrupt the story to back up and figure out who's talking now.

Also, for more than two speakers, be sure to indicate the speaker each time, and at the beginning is even better:

Gord jumped in. "What do you mean?"

7. Try to use action tags (beats) instead of dialogue tags, such as:

Shelley hung up the phone. "That was Carole."

Mark tensed. "What did she want?"

8. Avoid having the characters constantly using each other's names.

Once in a while is good, especially when they're greeting each other, but don't overdo it.

See also Chapter 25 – Dialogue Nuts and Bolts.

Chapter 24 – SOME MAJOR
DIALOGUE TURN-OFFS

Real-life conversation is no excuse for confusing, irritating, distracting, or boring dialogue coming out of your fiction characters' mouths.

First off, don't confuse, frustrate or annoy your readers by trying to reproduce regional dialects exactly as they sound.

Also, I'd be cautious about using the very latest slang expressions, which could backfire on you and end up dating your story within a year or two. That would not be cool!

And overloading dialogue with in-your-face profanities can lose you readers.

And finally, please, please, for all of us, leave out all the boring yadda-yadda, blah-blah "Nice weather" stuff!

DON'T MANGLE CHARACTERS' SPEECH

Don't make the mistake of trying to reproduce regional speech patterns phonetically. As Jack Bickham says, "There was a time, not so long ago, when fiction writers strove for authenticity in some of their stories by attempting to imitate regional and ethnic dialects and pronunciations by purposely misspelling words in their dialogue. Today such practices have fallen into disfavor."

Why? Because it's distracting and irritating. Not only that, it runs the risk of obscuring your intended meaning. All of which will result in taking your reader out of your story – the exact opposite effect you're going for. Also, you could easily end up offending people from that region if you depict their everyday casual language as a kind of inferior, laughable sublanguage.

Here's an example of what I mean, from an older story about slaves and the Civil War. The passage was narrated by a slave:

> So dey jump on dey horses an' gallop 'way. An' we ain't see'd dem since. Dey friends say dey be kilt in one o' de firs' battles o' de war. Dat be good lesson fo' we, shure 'nuf! Black folk ain't gonna go off ta fight in a war. Life be tuff enuf here wid' Massa an' his whip, widout uder buckra be shootin' at de menfolk an' killin' 'em dead.

And it went on like that for pages and pages! Ouch!

So these days, phonetic spelling, misspelling words to show different pronunciations, the overuse of apostrophes to indicate missing letters (unpronounced sounds), and other deviations from standard North American speech (for books set in the U.S. or Canada) are frowned upon by most editors, agents, and discerning readers, and may earn a rejection for your otherwise compelling story.

An occasional elision (dropped sound, indicated by an apostrophe) and plenty of regular contractions, with the odd regional word or expression thrown in for local color are usually enough to get your regional flavor across to your readers.

DON'T TRY TO KEEP UP WITH THE VERY LATEST SLANG EXPRESSIONS

Many new authors try to appeal to their audience by using the latest slang expressions, especially in YA fiction. This is usually a mistake. The language is changing so fast, especially fad expressions, that what's trendy or "in" today may be already dated by the time your short story or novel sees the light of day. For example, a writer from the 60s or early 70s who wanted to write a novel with universal appeal that would stand the test of time would really blow it by using expressions like "Groovy, man!"

The moral? Be careful with using cutting-edge slang expressions. It's usually best to stick to slang expressions that have been around for at least a few years.

DON'T OVERDO THE PROFANITIES

Another area where beginning writers mess up is in replicating every F-word in real life on their page, leaving many readers wincing. Profanities and obscenities can often slide by in real life, depending on the situation, but they usually jump out at us on the printed page, so use them judiciously, to get the general flavor, rather than on every line.

As Jack Bickham says, "Dirty talk often looks dirtier on the page than it actually is." So save the worst of your swear words for those story situations where a strong curse word is really needed to convey the emotion.

Also, consider your genre. Readers of cozy mysteries, for example, are mostly women aged sixty and up, so best to use less graphic language in those stories. The odd "Damn!" or "Crap!" will usually suffice.

DON'T REPRODUCE ACTUAL CONVERSATIONS VERBATIM

By this I mean all the *uhs* and *ums* and *ers* and *you knows* and "How are you?" "I'm fine, and you?" Not to mention introducing people, chitchat about the weather, and other empty social niceties that lead up to (or follow) the real meat of the conversation. That's a sure-fire recipe for putting your readers to sleep! And they won't be eager to pick up your book again when they wake up.

As Ingermanson and Economy say, "Dialogue is war!"

You need tension on every page, including in your dialogue. So if it doesn't drive the story forward, add conflict or tension, or contribute to character development, take it out.

DON'T LECTURE THROUGH MONOLOGUES

Avoid having one character pontificate or explain stuff for more than a short paragraph or two. This is both boring and unrealistic. Instead, pare down the information, turn it into a question and answer situation, and introduce some tension and attitude.

So, oddball spelling, attempts at reproducing regional dialects phonetically, and heavy use of profanities all risk offending someone, whether it's a member of a minority or someone who doesn't like swearing. And the latest slang expressions may soon appear outdated and ridiculous. And really, empty blah blah is boring, isn't it? So be wary of reproducing characters' dialogue exactly as it sounds in real life – it could backfire on you.

Resources:
Jack M. Bickham, *The 38 Most Common Fiction Writing Mistakes*
Randy Ingermanson and Peter Economy, *Writing Fiction for Dummies*
& Jodie's observations and editing experience

Chapter 25 – DIALOGUE NUTS & BOLTS

In the previous two chapters, I discussed various techniques for writing dialogue that comes alive on the page.

This chapter just provides a reference for the grammatically correct way to write dialogue, as well as some style tips for dialogue tags. Using correct punctuation and form for dialogue will keep your readers from becoming distracted, confused or annoyed, and maintain their focus on your story. So if you want your manuscript to look professional and your story to read smoothly, follow these technical guidelines.

THE BASICS

~ Paragraphing:

First of all, start a new paragraph every time the speaker changes. On the other hand, don't start a new paragraph if it's still the same speaker, unless you're doing it for a pause or emphasis.

Also, start a new paragraph for someone else reacting to the speaker's words or actions.

~ Punctuation and capitalization for dialogue:

1. Put quotation marks around all spoken words. Although in Britain and Australia, it's more common to use single quotes around dialogue, in the United States and Canada, the standard is **double quotes around dialogue**, with single quotes for quoting or emphasizing words or phrases within the quoted dialogue. (Italics are also used for emphasizing words or short phrases – but don't overdo it.)

2. In North America, the **punctuation always goes inside the end quote**, not outside it:

"What's wrong with you?" he asked.

"Nothing," she replied.

3. If the person is asking a question, the question mark goes inside the quotation mark, and a period goes at the end of the whole sentence. The same goes for exclamations.

"Where were you?" she asked.

"Help!" he shouted.

Note that in the above examples, even though your word processor wants you to put a capital letter for "she" or "he", these need to be lowercase, as they don't start a new sentence.

4. If the person speaking is making a statement (or a suggestion or a command), replace the period (which would follow if it weren't in quotation marks) with a comma. Then put your period at the end of the sentence.

"Let's go home," he said.

5. If there's no attribute (he said, she said), put a period inside the closing quotation mark.

"Turn off the TV."

6. If you start with the dialogue tag, put a comma after it, before your opening quotation mark and the dialogue:

He said, "But my game is on."

7. If you want to put your dialogue tag in the middle of a sentence, put a comma inside the first set of closing quotation marks, and also after the dialogue tag:

"I can never understand," she said, "what you see in him."

(Note no capital for the second part.)

8. If one person is speaking and the dialogue goes on for more than one paragraph (not a great idea to have one person speaking at great length), you leave out the closing quotation marks at the end of the first paragraph, but put opening quotation marks at the beginning of the next one. Use closing quotation marks only when that person is finished speaking.

"...no matter what you do.

"And another thing, don't ...."

STYLE TIPS FOR DIALOGUE

~ Avoid overusing dialogue tags. Leave them out sometimes or use an action beat instead.

Rather than constantly using *he said* or *she said* (or the name and said), omit them sometimes or replace them with an action beat, which will also help bring the scene alive. The action immediately before or after the words tells us who's talking.

She looked at him in alarm. "What do you mean?"

He ran his hand through his hair. "I have no idea."

"Where's Fluffy?" Chris opened the back door and looked around.

~ The best dialogue tags are the simple *he said* and *she said* (or asked), or with the name: John said, Carol said.

These simple dialogue tags don't draw attention to themselves or interrupt the story line, as they're almost invisible. Avoid fancy tags like *queried, chortled, alleged, proclaimed, conjectured,* etc. But I do suggest using verbs that accurately and quickly describe how the words are delivered, like *whispered, shouted* or *stammered.*

~ You can't use words like *laughed* or *grinned* or *smiled* or *grimaced* or *scowled* as dialogue tags:

Incorrect:

"You look great," he grinned.

"Why, thank you," she smiled.

Why not? Because smiling is not talking; you can't "smile" or "grin" words.

Change to:

"Why, thank you." She smiled at the compliment.

(Note period and capital "She")

Or:

"Why, thank you," she said, then smiled at him.

~ Use adverbs very sparingly.

Avoid:

"Come here," he said loudly.

"I'm in charge," she said haughtily.

The words they say should already express how they're feeling and how they're saying them.

~ And finally, a current style trend:

Contemporary North American fiction seems to avoid the reversed form, "said Joe," in favor of "Joe said." The reversed form seems to be more British and also considered kind of archaic.

This is just an observation, not a rule, but aspiring or debut authors would do well to stick with what seems to be in favor, to give a contemporary feel to your novel. Of course, if you're writing historical fiction, go for the older "said Elizabeth" form.

Chapter 26 – EXPRESSING
THOUGHT-REACTIONS IN FICTION

How do you express thoughts and inner reactions in fiction? Thoughts, like dialogue, need to drive the story forward and be natural-sounding and appropriate for both the "thinker" and the situation.

I've purposely used the term "thought-reactions," instead of just "thoughts," as in fiction, in any given scene, we're in someone's point of view, so in their head, privy to their thoughts. In that sense, all the narration for that scene is or should be in their thoughts, colored with their attitude, and written in ordinary font, with no special punctuation or thought tags.

For example, in Sandra Brown's *Ricochet*, we're in Duncan's point of view. We read:

> Within seconds Jenny appeared. All six feet of her, most of it sleek, tanned legs that looked like they'd been airbrushed to perfection.

This is obviously Duncan's viewpoint and his opinion/thoughts. No need to say "he thought."

Thought-reactions, on the other hand, are when that viewpoint character (and only the POV character – we shouldn't know the thoughts of anyone else in that scene) has an inner, emotional reaction to something that has just happened, or something someone has just said or done, whether it be anger, delight, confusion, frustration, surprise, or whatever. Or perhaps they're actively planning something.

In popular fiction written in third-person (he, she, they) past tense, you'll see thoughts or thought-reactions appearing in either present or past tense, in first-person (I), second-person (you), or third-person (he, she, they).

Indirect thoughts are expressed in third-person, past tense, normal font:

She wondered where she'd left her keys.

Direct thoughts are written in first-person, present tense, in either italics or normal font:

Where are those damn keys?

INDIRECT THOUGHTS

Indirect introspection or indirect thoughts summarize or paraphrase the thinker's words. **Indirect thoughts are usually expressed in third-person, past tense and written in normal font** (avoid italics for indirect thoughts), with or without thought tags, like "she thought" or "he thought." This is the equivalent to reporting what somebody said, rather than using their exact words in quotation marks, only of course these words are not spoken.

She hoped he wouldn't be late again.

Why couldn't she understand where he was coming from?

If he didn't know better, he would swear she was genuinely perplexed.

DIRECT THOUGHTS

Direct introspection or direct thoughts use the character's exact (unspoken) words, normally expressed in **first-person, present tense. They can be in normal font or in italics.** This is the equivalent to dialogue in quotation marks, except the words aren't spoken out loud.

Where the hell is he?

Why doesn't she get it?

I'd better call Mom today.

Where's that phone number?

Putting direct thoughts in italics can be very effective for expressing a sudden strong emotional reaction. Showing these visceral reactions of your characters helps us get inside their heads and hearts more deeply and bond with them more. Showing a thought-reaction in italics works best when used sparingly, for a significant or urgent thought or reaction:

Rats!

Omigod!

Leave out the thought tag, as the italics signify a direct thought, in this case.

EXAMPLES

Here are some examples of indirect thoughts contrasted with the same thought expressed directly.

Indirect: She felt lucky.

~ **Direct:** *Lucky me!*

Indirect: He was such an idiot.

~ **Direct:** *What an idiot!* Or, in second person: *You idiot!*

Indirect: She had to be kidding.

~ **Direct:** *What? You've got to be kidding!* (second person)

Indirect: Did she really think he'd believe that?

~ **Direct:** *Give me a break!*

Indirect: It was a gorgeous day.

~ **Direct:** What a gorgeous day. (Doesn't have to be in italics.)

Indirect: Jake took a step back, wondering what he'd done.

~ **Direct:** Jake took a step back. *Holy crap. What have I done?*

Here's an example from *Don't Look Twice*, by Andrew Gross:

> It was already after ten! She tried David's cell one more time. Again, his voice mail came on.
>
> *What the hell is going on, David?*
>
> She started to get worried....

NO-NO'S

~ **Never use quotation marks around thoughts.** Quotation marks designate spoken words.

~ **Never say "he thought to himself"** or "she thought to herself." That's a sign of amateurish writing—who else would they be thinking to?

~ **Don't have your characters think in complete sentences.** Expressing thoughts in perfect, grammatically correct, complex sentences is just not realistic. Many of our thoughts are emotional reactions, flashes or images, expressed through a few well-chosen words.

PART VI

WRAP-UP

Chapter 27 – TO RECAP: 20 STYLE BLUNDERS THAT CONFUSE, ANNOY, OR BORE YOUR READERS

Let's tie up this style guide with a review of some of the most glaring style gaffes to avoid in your fiction writing. I'm talking about those little errors and bad habits that creep into your manuscript, weaken your message, and add up to an overall feeling of amateurish writing.

Readers might not know exactly what it is in your writing style that's less than satisfying for them, but a general impression of mediocre prose instead of a stellar style can make them put the book down and either give it a bad review or just not recommend it to others.

The good news is that, unlike the more critical aspects of story plot and characterization, these little bad habits are easy to correct, resulting in a much more polished, compelling manuscript.

~ LOOSEN UP YOUR LANGUAGE.

For today's fiction, or even most nonfiction (blogs, websites, e-magazine and magazine articles), it's important to let go of those old overly-correct, lengthy formal sentence structures and stuffy-sounding words, and learn to write in a more relaxed, conversational tone. Or a terse, tense and fast-paced style, if the scene calls for it. For popular fiction and blogs, it's usually better to use short or medium-length sentences and paragraphs, and forego long, convoluted sentence structure and officious-sounding words and phrases like *inasmuch as, however, be that as it may, nonetheless, whom, whereby, insofar as*, etc.

~ AVOID AFFECTED OR PRETENTIOUS EXPRESSIONS.

Rather than impressing your readers, ostentatious words and phrases can just end up alienating them. Readers don't want to interrupt your story to look a word up in the dictionary. As Jessica Morrell points out, "Simple words are close to our hearts and easily understood…. simpler words are unpretentious, yet contain power and grace….Pompous words are alienating, boring, and outdated." So instead of "facilitated," use "helped"; instead of "What transpired that day?" say "What happened that day?" Instead of "The news proliferated," use "The news spread"; and instead of "he was prevaricating," say "he was lying." See chapter 16.

~ BUT BAN THOSE OVERUSED, TRITE WORDS, AND CUT BACK ON THE CLICHES.

Excise those tired, overdone words that have lost all power to excite, like *good, bad, nice, happy, sad, big, small, tall, short, old, young, pretty, kind, walked, ran,* and *looked.* Get out your thesaurus or go to thesaurus.com and find a fresher, more vibrant word that captures the image or mood more precisely and brings the situation to life. And use a specific noun over a generic one. Instead of "flowers," tell what kind of flowers; instead of "a bird" say "an eagle" or "a seagull," etc.

Also, be on the lookout for any expressions you've used that have been flogged to death, like "hard as nails," "skinny as a broom," "smart as a whip," "blind as a bat," or "dead as a doornail." Find a fresh way to bring the feeling or sensation to life.

~ SHOW, DON'T TELL.

Show us, don't tell us how your characters are feeling. Avoid "was" statements like "She was depressed," "He found that funny," or "I was angry," or "The little girl felt sad." Show these emotions by their actions, words, and body language: "Eyes downcast, shoulders slumped, she silently pushed the food around her plate." See Chapter 3 for more on this.

~ WATCH FOR WORDINESS AND FOREGO FILLER PHRASES.

Don't clutter up your sentences with a lot of extra little words. For example, instead of writing *in the vicinity of,* just write *near.* Instead of *as a consequence of,* just write *because.* Instead of *a large percentage of,* just use *many.* Instead of *located at,* just say *at.*

Also, take out empty phrases like "There is," "There was," "There were," "It's," "It was." Jump right in with what you're actually talking about.

~ FERRET OUT THOSE PET PHRASES AND FIND FRESH IMAGERY.

For this, you'll probably need a second set of eyes to spot those pet phrases or imagery you don't realize you're constantly repeating. Imagery like variations on "She caught her breath" or "She couldn't breathe" or "She had trouble catching her breath" or "She held her breath." Figure out other ways to show her apprehension. A good resource for emotions and reactions for each situation is *The Emotion Thesaurus.* Whether you're describing the setting, the weather, or the hero or heroine, vary your wording and imagery. See Chapters 21 and 22 for more on this.

~ REJECT REPETITIONS

Avoid repeating the same word or family of words within the same paragraph or page, e.g., *help, helpless, helpful, unhelpful, helplessly*; or *happy, unhappy, happily, unhappily, happiness*, etc. Look for a completely different word to express the same thing.

~ TAKE OUT WISHY-WASHY QUALIFIERS.

Find and take out modifiers that weaken your prose, like *quite, sort of, almost, kind of, a bit, pretty, somewhat, mildly, rather, usually, basically, generally, probably, mostly, really,* and *very.* Forget "He was quite brave," or "She was pretty intelligent" or "It was almost scary," or "It was mildly frightening."

These qualifiers dilute your message, reduce the impact, and make the imagery weaker. Delete them. Even *very* is to be avoided – it's like you're saying the following word needs reinforcing. "She was beautiful" packs more punch than "She was very beautiful."

A quick, simple way to ferret out these weak words is your "Find and Replace" tool. You can start by doing a search for these words: *quite, very, that, suddenly, immediately, now*, and *then*, and taking out many or most of them. See Chapter 14 for more on this.

~ AVOID COLORLESS, OVERUSED VERBS.

Banish overdone, blah verbs like *walked, ran, went, saw, talked, ate, did, got, put, took, turned*. Get out your thesaurus or use the MS Word one. (Hint: look up the present tense: walk, run, eat, say, etc.) to find more expressive, powerful verbs instead, like *crept, loped, stumbled, stomped, glimpsed, noticed, observed, witnessed, spied, grunted, whimpered, devoured, consumed, gobbled, wolfed, munched, bolted, raged*, or *grabbed*. See Chapter 21 for more on this.

~ FOR MORE POWER, AVOID -ING VERBS WHENEVER POSSIBLE.

Use -ed verbs instead – they're stronger and more immediate. "He was racing" is weaker than "He raced." "They searched the house" is more forceful and immediate than "They were searching the house." Rewrite -ing verbs whenever you can, and you'll strengthen your writing and increase its power.

But use -ing verbs when needed for background or ongoing action.
You need –ing verbs for a continuous action, one that's already taking place when something else happens. For example, "When we found the house, a man was washing a car in the driveway." Or "Christy was heading out the door when the phone rang."

~ KEEP ADVERBS TO A MINIMUM.

Instead of propping up a boring, anemic verb with an adverb, look for strong, descriptive, powerful verbs. Instead of "He walked slowly," go for "He plodded" or "He trudged" or "He dawdled." Instead of "She ate hungrily," say "She devoured the bag of chips," or "She wolfed down the pizza." Instead of "They talked quickly," say "They babbled" or "They chattered" or "They gossiped."

~ USE ADJECTIVES SPARINGLY.

Instead of stringing a bunch of adjectives in front of an ordinary, overused noun, find a more precise, expressive noun to show rather than tell. Overuse of adjectives can also turn your writing into "purple prose" that is melodramatic and overly "flowery." And a pile-up of adjectives in front of a noun gives a delayed meaning while the reader slugs through all of them before discovering the most important thing – the noun they're modifying. I picked up a plump, red, juicy, mouthwatering….tomato? strawberry? peach? plum?

~ VARY THE LENGTH AND STRUCTURE OF YOUR SENTENCES.

Use a combination of short, long, and medium-length sentences, as well as the occasional one- or two-word sentences. Mix it up! Longer, more involved sentences suit thoughtful, analytical or dreamy times, and short, terse sentences are great for stressful times. One-word sentences are great for dialogue, especially if the speaker is a man. See Chapter 18.

Don't start sentence after sentence with a name or he/she/I/we/they (subject – verb), as that can get monotonous to read. For example, avoid:

> Carole pulled her car into the parking lot and found a parking space. She got out and hurried into the restaurant. She looked around for her friends and spied them at a table in the corner. She hurried over to join them. She saw her ex-husband at a table with an attractive woman.

Instead, change up your sentences to add interest and variety:

> Carole found a parking space and hurried into the restaurant. Looking around, she spied her friends at a table in the corner. As she hurried over to join them, she noticed her ex-husband at a table with an attractive woman.

Similarly, don't start sentence after sentence with -ing or -ed verbs (participles), as in:

Paying the bill, he smiled at her. Delighted, she started feeling the date was going well. Tossing her hair back, she returned his smile. Picking up her purse, she searched for her lipstick. Pushing back her chair, she….

(Exaggerated for effect, but you get the picture.)

More on this in Chapter 18.

~ REWRITE THAT BORING, STILTED DIALOGUE.

Dialogue needs to be casual and natural-sounding. Avoid overly correct, perfectly formed sentences. Use incomplete sentences, one- or two-word questions and answers, lots of contractions (I'll, won't, etc.), and slang expressions. Also, avoid the blah-blah mundane niceties ("Hi, how are you?" "I'm fine, and you?" and jump straight to the meaningful stuff. Dialogue needs lots of conflict, tension and attitude!

~ STICK WITH BASIC DIALOGUE TAGS OR USE AN ACTION BEAT INSTEAD.

To tell who's speaking, use mostly *he said* and *she said* (or *asked*) wherever possible, rather than show-offy sounding alternates like *emphasized, reiterated, questioned, uttered, conjecture, queried, articulated, declared, asserted,* etc. These synonyms for "said" might seem more imaginative or precise, but the problem is they stand out, so they take the reader out of the story, whereas "said" is almost invisible.

However, I like dialogue tags that describe *how* something is said, as in *he shouted, she murmured, he grumbled, she whispered, he stuttered, she muttered, he yelled.*

You can often eliminate the dialogue tag altogether and just use an action beat to show who's talking:

He picked up the phone. "That's it. I'm calling the cops."

~ TO AVOID CONFUSION, DESCRIBE THE STIMULUS, THEN THE RESPONSE.

Show the action before the reaction. When writing an action scene, make sure your sentence structure mimics the order of the actions. The reader pictures the actions in the order that she reads them, so it's confusing to read about the reaction before finding out what caused it.

So describe the action first, then the reaction: Instead of "She screamed when the door slammed on her finger," write: "The door slammed on her finger and she screamed." (Or "causing her to scream," or whatever.) See Chapter 6 for more on this.

~ FOR GREATER IMPACT, AVOID THE PASSIVE VOICE.

When describing an action, it's more effective to start with the doer, then describe what he or she did, rather than the other way around. Use the more direct active voice wherever possible, for more impact.

Instead of "The crime scene was taped off by the police," write "The police taped off the crime scene."

Instead of "The soccer ball was kicked by the boy," write "The boy kicked the soccer ball."

~ SAY NO TO NEGATIVE CONSTRUCTIONS.

Double negatives especially can be confusing to the reader, and you don't want anything to stand between them and your story. Instead of "I didn't disagree with him," say "I agreed with him." Instead of "She wasn't unhappy," say "She was happy."

~ MANAGE THOSE MISPLACED MODIFIERS.

Keep on the lookout for awkward constructions like: "A cheerful matronly type, Doug followed the housekeeper into the room." The construction of this sentence implies that Doug is the matronly type, when it's the housekeeper. Same problem with, "Tall and rugged, Jane thought he was just her type." Jane's not the one who's tall and rugged, but this sentence implies that she is. Savvy readers will find these laughable and dismiss you as an amateur. See Chapter 17 for more on this.

~ DON'T OVERDO THE EXCLAMATION POINTS!

Use exclamation points very sparingly – less than ten for your whole novel is a good guideline. But do use them where they're needed, like for someone screaming, yelling, shocked, or in pain, eg. "Help!" or "Stop!" or "Mommy!"

Resources:
Jodie's editing, and
Elizabeth Lyon, *Manuscript Makeover*
Howard Mittelmark and Sandra Newman, *How NOT to Write a Novel*
Jessica Page Morrell, *Thanks, But This Isn't For Us*

YOU BE THE EDITOR

Now it's your turn. Grab a piece of paper and using the tips you've picked up from this book, edit the examples below to make them tighter, more powerful, more compelling, and tenser. Then look for possible solutions at the bottom.

~ **Streamlining:** How would you fix these awkward, overly wordy sentences to improve the pacing and flow?

(1) Allan recommenced after the abrupt interruption, with a scowl in the direction of its origin.

(2) "Excuse us for a moment," Janet said, through clenched teeth. When they were far enough from the group that they could speak without being heard, she whispered, "What the hell are you doing?

~ **Writing Tense Action Scenes:** Rewrite this passage to make it tighter and tenser:

(3) An inline skater came careening around the corner and skated fast towards them, shouting loudly. Josh shot a look back at Amy as he grabbed her arm and pulled her bodily to the edge of the street out of the path of the oncoming skater.

~ **Don't Overexplain:** Can you take out a sentence or two?

(4) A shudder cascaded through her body. Denise felt her entire body go ice cold, as shock gripped her. She was colder than she had ever been in her entire life. It felt as if she had stepped into a refrigerator, as shivers racked her body.

148

~ State actions in the order they occur: Rephrase this to fix the order.

(5) He grabbed her and threw her into the kitchen. That was the last thing she remembered after hitting her head on the corner of the counter.

~ Show, Don't Tell: Take out the "tell" and rephrase a bit.

(6) The two men were strong. They picked up George as if he were a large sack of potatoes and threw him out the door.

~ Fix these sentences:

(7) Karen swiveled her head around and saw Keith walk in the door.

(8) Shoveling the snow, Mary watched her son out in the driveway.

(9) Cathy walked into the ward. Before her eyes landed on the patient, she heard the blaring of a television set.

~ Replace each phrase with one word:

(10) spoke in a muffled fashion –

(11) in spite of the fact that –

(12) during the time that –

(13) for the simple reason that –

~ Take out all unnecessary words and combine to make one sentence:

(14) We passed a huge towering old run-down mansion located on a deserted street with no one around. The house was brown in color.

(15) The sword that he was holding was knocked to the ground.

YOU BE THE EDITOR – POSSIBLE SOLUTIONS:

~ Streamlining:

(1) Mike scowled at the interruption, then continued.

(2) "Excuse us for a moment," Janet said, through clenched teeth. When they were out of earshot, she whispered, "What the hell are you doing?

~ Writing Action Scenes:

(3) An inline skater came careening around the corner and barreled towards them, yelling. Josh grabbed Amy's arm and yanked her out of the way.

~ Don't Overexplain:

(4) A shudder cascaded through her body. Denise felt her entire body go ice cold, as shock gripped her. As shivers racked her body, it felt as if she had stepped into a refrigerator.

~ State actions in the order they occur:

(5) He grabbed her and threw her into the kitchen. She hit her head on the corner of the counter and everything went black.

~ Show, Don't Tell:

(6) The two burly men picked up George as if he were a huge sack of potatoes and threw him out the door.

~ Fix these sentences:

(7) Karen turned and saw Keith walk in the door. (or "turned to see")

(8) Mary watched her son shoveling snow out in the driveway.

(9) Cathy walked into the ward. Before she saw (or "she noticed") the patient, she heard the blaring of a television set.

~ **Replace each phrase with one word:**

(10) spoke in a muffled fashion – mumbled

(11) in spite of the fact that – although

(12) during the time that – while

(13) for the simple reason that – because

~ **Take out all unnecessary words:**

(14) We passed a huge brown run-down mansion on a deserted street.

(15) His sword was knocked to the ground.

A FEW WORDS FROM THE AUTHOR

I'd love to hear from you. If my advice here has inspired you and provided you with some concrete, useable tips to help make your story more compelling and sellable by amping up your opening, polishing up your writing style, fine-tuning the pace, and developing your authentic voice, I'd really appreciate it if you could write a short review of this book on its Amazon page.

And if you have any questions or suggestions for this or future books, please email me at: info@JodieRennerEditing.com. Thanks!

And do check out my e-booklet, *Writing a Killer Thriller – An Editor's Guide to Writing Powerful Fiction*. It's compact, highly skimmable, and full of great tips for increasing the conflict, suspense and intrigue of any novel, not just thrillers.

I will soon be publishing more books on other aspects of writing compelling fiction, such as characterization, point of view, scene structure, and grammar, so I hope you'll check back to my Amazon Author Page regularly to look for them.

Also, please email me with any questions or suggestions for fiction-writing or editing topics you'd like me to address in future books.

And I look forward to reading your published fiction!

~ Jodie Renner, www.JodieRennerEditing.com, March 2013

ABOUT THE AUTHOR

Jodie Renner is a freelance fiction editor who specializes in thrillers, romantic suspense, mysteries, and other crime fiction, as well as mainstream, young adult, and historical fiction.

Jodie has a master's degree in literature, taught English for many years, was a librarian for two years, and continues her lifelong passion for reading well-written, compelling fiction. Some of Jodie's current favorite authors include Robert Crais, Sandra Brown, Lee Child, Lisa Gardner, Michael Connelly, Allison Brennan, Harlan Coben, and Nora Roberts.

Jodie's author clients contact her from all over the world, but most are in the U.S, especially the West Coast and Eastern Seaboard. For more information on Jodie's editing services or books, or to contact her, please visit www.JodieRennerEditing.com or www.JodieRenner.com.

To read Jodie's articles on various aspects of writing compelling fiction, please visit Jodie's group blog, *Crime Fiction Collective*. Jodie's craft-of-writing articles are also published on various other blogs, including *The Writer's Forensics Blog*, *The Thrill Begins*, *The Kill Zone*, *Blood-Red Pencil*, and her own blog, *Jodie Renner Editing*. Look for more craft-of-fiction books by Jodie in 2013.

When she's not editing fiction or reading novels or craft-of-writing books, Jodie loves to pursue her two other main passions, traveling and photography. In fact, Jodie loves traveling so much she's thinking of changing her tagline from "Let's work together to enhance and empower your writing," to "Have laptop, will travel."

SOME EXCELLENT RESOURCES
FOR FICTION WRITERS:

A. Recommended by Jodie Renner:

Writing Fiction for Dummies, by Randy Ingermanson & Peter Economy. Not for dummies at all! Covers all the basics for aspiring novelists.

Revision & Self-Editing – Techniques for transforming your first draft into a finished novel, by James Scott Bell. An excellent guide for making your story more compelling.

Manuscript Makeover – Revision Techniques No Fiction Writer Can Afford to Ignore, by Elizabeth Lyon

The Everything Guide to Writing Your First Novel, by Hallie Ephron

The 38 Most Common Fiction Writing Mistakes (And How to Avoid Them), by Jack M. Bickham. Great tips – short and to the point!

Conflict & Suspense, by James Scott Bell. Turn your novel into a real page-turner!

Thanks, But This Isn't For Us, by Jessica Page Morrell. Jam-packed with invaluable advice for writing a novel that will captivate and sell.

Between the Lines – the subtle elements of fiction writing, by Jessica Page Morrell

The Emotion Thesaurus – A Writer's Guide to Character Expression, by Angela Ackerman and Becca Puglisi. An excellent resource for nailing character reactions.

Stein on Writing, by Sol Stein

Writing the Breakout Novel, by Donald Maass. All-around great. Look for the accompanying workbook.

How to Write a Damn Good Novel, by James N. Frey
How to Write a Damn Good Thriller, by James N. Frey
How to Write a Damn Good Mystery, by James N. Frey

The Successful Novelist, by David Morrell. Great advice from a bestselling author!

Self-Editing for Fiction Writers – How to Edit Yourself into Print, by Renni Browne and Dave King

B. Well-Respected Craft of Writing Books, Listed Alphabetically by Author:

Bell, James Scott, *Revision & Self-Editing – Techniques for transforming your first draft into a finished novel*
Bell, James Scott, *Conflict & Suspense*
Bell, James Scott, *Plot & Structure*
Bell, James Scott, *The War of Writing*

Bickham, Jack M., *The 38 Most Common Fiction Writing Mistakes (And How to Avoid Them)*

Bradbury, Ray, *Zen in the Art of Writing: Releasing the Creative Genius Within You*

Browne, Renni and Dave King, *Self-Editing for Fiction Writers – How to Edit Yourself into Print*

Card, Orson Scott, *Characters & Viewpoint – Elements of Fiction Writing*

Ephron, Hallie, *The Everything Guide to Writing Your First Novel*

Frey, James N., *How to Write a Damn Good Novel*
Frey, James N., *How to Write a Damn Good Thriller*
Frey, James N., *How to Write a Damn Good Mystery*

Gardner, John, *On Becoming a Novelist*

Goldberg, Natalie, *Writing Down the Bones*

Ingermanson, Randy & Peter Economy, *Writing Fiction for Dummies*

King, Stephen, *On Writing – A Memoir of the Craft*

Lamott, Anne, *Bird by Bird, Some Instructions on Writing and Life*

Lukeman, Noah, *The First Five Pages – A Writer's Guide to Staying out of the Rejection Pile*

Lyon, Elizabeth, *Manuscript Makeover – Revision Techniques No Fiction Writer Can Afford to Ignore*
Lyon, Elizabeth, *A Writer's Guide to Fiction*

Maass, Donald, *Writing the Breakout Novel*
Maass, Donald, *The Fire in Fiction*

McKee, Robert, *Story: Substance, Structure, Style, and the Principles of Screenwriting*

Morrell, Jessica Page, *Thanks, But This Isn't For Us, A (Sort of) Compassionate Guide to Why Your Writing is Being Rejected*
Morrell, Jessica Page, *Between the Lines – the subtle elements of fiction writing*

Morrell, David, *The Successful Novelist*

Stein, Sol, *Stein on Writing*

Swain, Dwight V., *Techniques of the Selling Writer*

Wiesner, Karen S., *From First Draft to Finished Novel*

Appendix 1: SCENE OUTLINE FORM

Creating a Scene Outline for Your Novel

First, what's a scene?

Although most novels are divided into chapters, the scene is actually the basic, most important unit of fiction. A modern novel normally has several dozen scenes. Each scene can range in length from a few paragraphs to a dozen pages or more. A chapter can contain one scene or several. A scene can be divided up among chapters, stopping at a critical moment for effect, with other scenes interwoven in the chapters in between.

Using the Scene Outline:

The outline below will help you organize your scenes and see if any of them need to be moved, revised, amped up, or cut.

This is a great tool for both "plotters" and "pantsers." Plotters/outliners can use it to outline your scenes early on in the process, and those of you who prefer to just let the words flow and write "by the seat of your pants" can use it later, to make sure the timeline makes sense and the scene has conflict/tension and a change.

Keep each scene description to a minimum. Don't get carried away with too many details, or the task could become arduous. The most important thing is the viewpoint character's goal for that scene, and what's preventing him/her from reaching that goal, plus any new conflicts / problems / questions that arise.

And you can use a different font color or highlight color for each POV (point of view) character, for quick reference.

If in doubt as to who should be the viewpoint character for that scene, most often it's your protagonist. Can also, less often, be your antagonist or another main character. It's almost never a minor character. If you can't decide who should be the POV character for a particular scene, go with the character who has the most invested emotionally or the most to lose in that scene.

SCENE OUTLINE:

Scene 1: Chapter: 1   Place: Date/Month/Season: Year
(approx.):

POV character: Other main characters:

POV character's goal here:

Main problem / conflict – Who/What is preventing MC from reaching
his/her goal:

Outcome – Usually a setback / new problem:

(And/or new info, revelation, new question, resolution of problem
[rarely]):

Scene 2: Chapter: Place: Date/Month/Season: Year
(approx.):

POV character: Other main characters:

POV character's goal:

Main problem/conflict/question:

Outcome (most often a setback):

Scene 3: Etc. Continue for as many scenes as you have.

Then print this up and cut the scenes apart, so you can rearrange them to
play around with your structure, or even take some out to see what you're
left with. If you've highlighted every POV character with a different
color, that will help you see at a glance how many scenes you have in
each character's point of view.

22682601R00093

Made in the USA
Charleston, SC
26 September 2013